Mel Bay Presents

# TEXAS STYLE FIDDLIN' WORKSHOP

## 51 TEXAS-STYLE TUNES ARRANGED FOR THE INTERMEDIATE LEVEL FIDDLER

## by Jeanine R. Orme

Online Audio

### ONLINE AUDIO

| | | |
|---|---|---|
| 1. Natchez Under the Hill | 18. Pacific Slope | 35. Redbird Hornpipe |
| 2. Poor Girl's Waltz | 19. Cincinnati Rag | 36. I Don't Love Nobody |
| 3. Red Apple Rag | 20. Bill Cheatum | 37. Sally Ann |
| 4. Blue Eagle | 21. Hot Foot | 38. Shortnin' Bread |
| 5. Molly Bloom | 22. Westphalia Waltz | 39. Beaumont Rag |
| 6. Fort Smith | 23. Hot Springs | 40. Wild John |
| 7. Martha Campbell | 24. George Booker | 41. Velvet's Waltz |
| 8. Peacock Rag | 25. Little Betty Brown | 42. Shuckin' the Bush |
| 9. Rickett's Hornpipe | 26. Ostinello Reel | 43. Cotton Patch Rag |
| 10. Blackberry Blossom | 27. Miller's Reel | 44. Crafton's Blues |
| 11. Here and There | 28. Cabri Waltz | 45. Durang's Hornpipe |
| 12. Richmond Polka | 29. Choctaw | 46. Eva Ann Waltz |
| 13. Old Sport | 30. Indian See-Saw | 47. Leather Britches |
| 14. Fiddler's Dream | 31. Coming Down from Denver | 48. Topeka Polka |
| 15. Paddy on the Turnpike | 32. Wagoner Hornpipe | 49. Waltz of Shannon |
| 16. Georgiana Moon | 33. Smith's Reel | 50. Tom & Jerry |
| 17. Fisher's Hornpipe | 34. Sixteen Days in Georgia | 51. High Level Hornpipe |

## To Access the Online Audio Go To:
## www.melbay.com/20315BCDEB

1 2 3 4 5 6 7 8 9 0

© 2008 BY MEL BAY PUBLICATIONS, INC., PACIFIC, MO 63069.
ALL RIGHTS RESERVED. INTERNATIONAL COPYRIGHT SECURED. B.M.I. MADE AND PRINTED IN U.S.A.
No part of this publication may be reproduced in whole or in part, or stored in a retrieval system, or transmitted in any form or by any means, electronic, mechanical, photocopy, recording, or otherwise, without written permission of the publisher.

**Visit us on the Web at www.melbay.com — E-mail us at email@melbay.com**

# Contents

| | |
|---|---|
| Introduction .................................................. 3 | George Booker ............................................ 34 |
| About the Author ........................................ 3 | Little Betty Brown ...................................... 35 |
| Overview of Musical Symbols and Style ...... 4 | Ostinello Reel ............................................. 36 |
| Fiddle Bowing ............................................. 5 | Miller's Reel ............................................... 37 |
| About Fiddle Contests ................................ 6 | Cabri Waltz ................................................ 38 |
| Natchez Under the Hill ............................... 7 | Choctaw ..................................................... 40 |
| Poor Girl's Waltz ......................................... 8 | Indian See Saw ........................................... 41 |
| Red Apple Rag ............................................ 9 | Coming Down From Denver ...................... 42 |
| Blue Eagle ................................................. 10 | Wagoner Hornpipe .................................... 43 |
| Molly Bloom .............................................. 11 | Smith's Reel ............................................... 44 |
| Fort Smith ................................................. 12 | Sixteen Days in Georgia ............................. 46 |
| Martha Campbell ...................................... 13 | Redbird Hornpipe ...................................... 47 |
| Peacock Rag .............................................. 14 | I Don't Love Nobody ................................. 48 |
| Rickett's Hornpipe .................................... 16 | Sally Ann ................................................... 50 |
| Blackberry Blossom .................................. 17 | Shortnin' Bread ......................................... 52 |
| Here and There ......................................... 18 | Beaumont Rag ........................................... 54 |
| Richmond Polka ........................................ 19 | Wild John .................................................. 56 |
| Old Sport .................................................. 20 | Velvet's Waltz ............................................ 58 |
| Fiddler's Dream ........................................ 21 | Shuckin' the Bush ...................................... 60 |
| Paddy on the Turnpike .............................. 22 | Cotton Patch Rag ....................................... 62 |
| Georgiana Moon ....................................... 23 | Crafton's Blues .......................................... 64 |
| Fisher's Hornpipe ...................................... 24 | Durang's Hornpipe .................................... 66 |
| Pacific Slope ............................................. 25 | Eva Ann Waltz ........................................... 68 |
| Cincinnati Rag .......................................... 26 | Leather Britches ........................................ 70 |
| Bill Cheatum ............................................. 27 | Topeka Polka ............................................. 72 |
| Hot Foot ................................................... 28 | Waltz of Shannon ...................................... 74 |
| Westphalia Waltz ...................................... 30 | Tom and Jerry ............................................ 76 |
| Hot Springs ............................................... 32 | High Level Hornpipe .................................. 79 |

# Acknowledgements

Special thanks to Herman Johnson for his many years of teaching me fiddle tunes. Thank you also to Clara Murphy, Helen Rabe, Jason Orme, John Stewart, Jeff Heberle, Frank Moore, Bob Heineth and Susy Spencer for their help with the completion and proof-reading of the book. Also, I would like to thank Andy Emert and Darol Anger for their help in producing the recording.

# Introduction

This book was written to be used as a learning tool and a reference for intermediate level fiddle players who have note reading ability. It presents tunes with workable bowing and fingering, and progresses in difficulty with each tune. This book provides information about bowing styles and playing in fiddle contests. Many of the tunes are in the style of Herman Johnson, a five-time National Fiddle Champion, as well as other great fiddlers.

Each fiddle tune can be played in many ways, and each fiddler has a different interpretation of how a song should be played. Interpreting fiddle music by a book alone is difficult. Using the compact disc that is available with this book will be helpful for understanding the bowings and the style of the tunes.

# About the Author

Jeanine Orme was born in Ogden, Utah. She began playing the violin at age five and started fiddling at age eight. She began playing with the Utah Old-Time Fiddlers and entered her first fiddle contest at age eleven. She has competed and served as a judge at the Weiser National Old-Time Fiddle contest, as well as other regional and state contests. She is a past Utah State Champion and Oregon State Adult Champion.

Her music has been influenced significantly by Herman Johnson who has instructed her in Texas-style fiddling and Western swing.

Jeanine has been teaching fiddle lessons for over twenty-five years. She has also played fiddle, bluegrass, and swing music in various bands in Utah and Oregon. She is the author of "The Fiddlin' Workshop" and "Herman Johnson Master Fiddler," Mel Bay Publications Inc. Jeanine and her husband reside in Oregon and she is the mother of three children.

# Overview of Musical Symbols and Style

*sl.* **Slide the finger** - This marking indicates that a slide adds to the style of the song.

◇A◇ **Section marking**

♪ **Grace note** - Ornamental note with no value by itself. Slur quickly into the next note.

**Tenuto sign** - Slight accent

> **Accent sign** - Play note with emphasis.

❜ **Pause**

 **Double stop** - 4th finger and open string are played together.

**Fingering** - Finger numbers are indicated when correct fingering makes a difference in the ease of playing or adds to the style of the song.

**Shifting** - A shift to third position is marked with correct fingering.

**Guitar Chords** - The guitar chords presented in this collection are basic and usable. Many variations or additional chords could be added. Texas-style guitar accompaniment adds passing chords and a running bass line. **Chords are only listed once when sections are the same.** Chords in parentheses ( ) are optional.

**Bowing Interpretation** - The bowing style for this collection is based on a pattern of three-note slurs. When you use a three-note slur, the bow direction does not change. Each phrase usually begins on a down bow. This style of bowing will generally have a smooth flow of notes, not rough or choppy.

**Swing rhythm** - Many fiddle tunes (including waltzes) should be played with an implied swing rhythm or syncopation on the eighth notes. Playing the eighth notes as written will not be the correct interpretation of style on those songs that are labeled as swing rhythm. A swing rhythm is approximated in the example below.

Swing Rhythm Exanple:

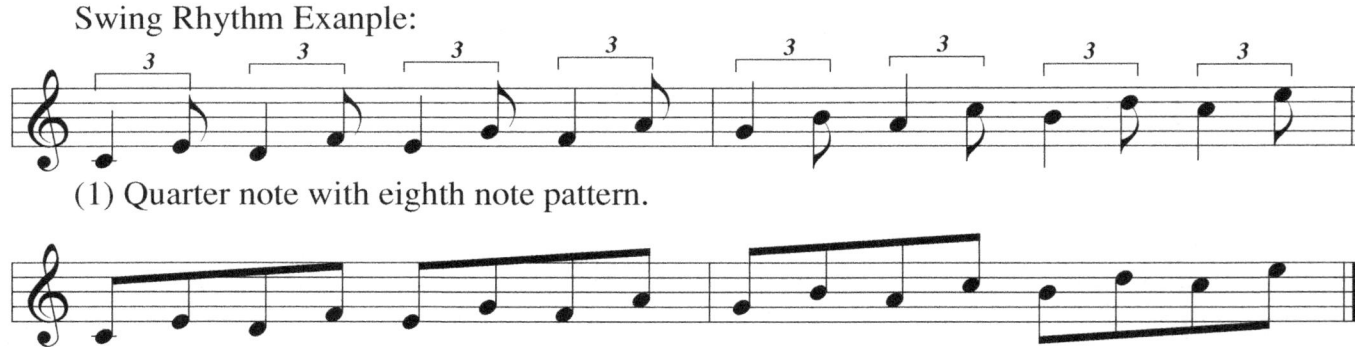

(1) Quarter note with eighth note pattern.

(2) Swing Rhythm, play as written above.

# Tips on Fiddle Bowing

I have always thought that the hardest thing to learn about fiddle playing is how to use the bow. By watching a player's bowing I can usually determine their ability level, whether they are classically trained on the violin, and the style of music that they play.

I have developed a style of bowing for my own playing mostly by watching great contest fiddlers. I have observed that fiddlers generally play with a very loose bow. My bow is usually loose enough that when I bear down on the bow, the hair will touch the wood of the bow. You don't want to loosen the bow to the point that you sound like you are playing on the wood instead of the hair of the bow. Playing with the bow loose keeps it from bouncing and I can get a much smoother flow of notes. Double stops are also much easier to play.

The next skill to develop is a very flexible wrist on the bow hand. It is more difficult to get any speed if you play with a stiff wrist. The best way to practice this skill is to play an easy fiddle tune like "Devil's Dream" and concentrate on bowing with the wrist. You may want to have someone hold on to your arm to force you to play only with the wrist. When you are used to playing with the wrist, then incorporate the wrist and arm movement together. You will use wrist and arm movement when you are playing a tune that is slower and needs longer bow strokes. You will use more wrist movement on passages that are very fast. It is helpful to play in the middle of your bow on fast passages.

Another problem in bowing is knowing when to slur notes together. I generally slur in a pattern of three-notes in a stroke. When you use a pattern of two-note slurs (See Ex. 1), it sounds too planned, and if you miss a slur it changes your bow direction. A pattern of three-note slurs on selected passages (See Ex. 2), sounds smoother and does not affect your bow direction. Another general rule is to always start a new phrase with a down bow to accent the first beat. The way to tell if your bow direction is backward is to see if you are starting phrases with a down bow or an up bow.

Example 1 - Two note slur pattern.

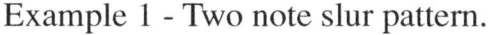

Example 2 - Three note slur pattern.

# About Fiddle Contests

For those who play the fiddle, but have never played in a fiddle contest, this information will help answer questions about how contests work.

In most contests, like the Weiser National Oldtime Fiddle Contest, the contestant must play a hoedown, a waltz, and a tune of choice in each round. Fiddle music is dance music, so the tunes should be danceable.

A hoedown can be difficult to define, but a tune which is called a breakdown, hornpipe, or reel would be considered a hoedown. It should be played in 2/4 or 4/4 time signature and should have strict eight-bar phrases. A hoedown is generally played faster than the tune of choice.

A fiddle waltz is any danceable waltz played in a fiddle style. A fiddle style waltz can have vibrato, but the vibrato should be slow and controlled rather than a fast classical vibrato.

A tune other than a hoedown or a waltz would be a tune of choice. Any rag, polka, jig, or a song in 6/8 time is appropriate if it is played in a fiddle style and at a danceable tempo. A tune that has 12-bar or 16-bar phrases would be considered to be a tune of choice.

Some general rules apply to most contests. There is no cross tuning allowed on stage and in most cases "trick or fancy fiddling" such as shuffle bowing is not allowed unless it is part of the original tune, not just added for show. Most judges will be listening for rhythm, tone quality, oldtime fiddling ability, and danceability when scoring a fiddle contest.

Fiddle contests rules vary wherever you go. It is a good idea to get familiar with the rules of a contest before you play in it. If you have any questions, ask the judges or other fiddlers. Fiddle contests are great places to meet new people and learn new tunes.

Most of the songs in "Texas Style Fiddlin' Workshop" would be appropriate for contests. The songs could be put into categories as follows:

| **Hoedown** | | **Waltz** | **Tune of Choice** |
|---|---|---|---|
| Natchez Under the Hill | Pacific Slope | Poor Girl's Waltz | Red Apple Rag |
| Blue Eagle | Ostinello Reel | Westphalia Waltz | Peacock Rag |
| Molly Bloom | Indian See-Saw* | Georgiana Moon | Richmond Polka* |
| Fort Smith | Wagoner Hornpipe | Cabri Waltz | Cincinnati Rag |
| Martha Campbell | Coming Down From Denver | Waltz of Shannon | Hot Foot |
| Blackberry Blossom | Smith's Reel | Eva Ann Waltz | Sixteen Days in Georgia |
| Paddy on the Turnpike | Redbird Hornpipe | Velvet's Waltz | I Don't Love Nobody |
| Here and There | Sally Ann | | Beaumont Rag |
| Wild John | Shortnin' Bread | | Cotton Patch Rag |
| Old Sport | High Level Hornpipe | | Crafton Blues |
| Fiddler's Dream | Bill Cheatum | | Topeka Polka |
| Fisher's Hornpipe | Shuckin' the Bush | | |
| Choctaw | Miller's Reel | | |
| Hot Springs* | Durang's Hornpipe | | |
| George Booker | Leather Britches | | |
| Little Betty Brown* | Tom & Jerry | | |

* There may be some question whether these tunes fit in the category of a hoedown or tune of choice. Inquire with a judge before you play these in a contest.

# Natchez Under the Hill

This tune is named after the city of Natchez, Mississippi.

Traditional

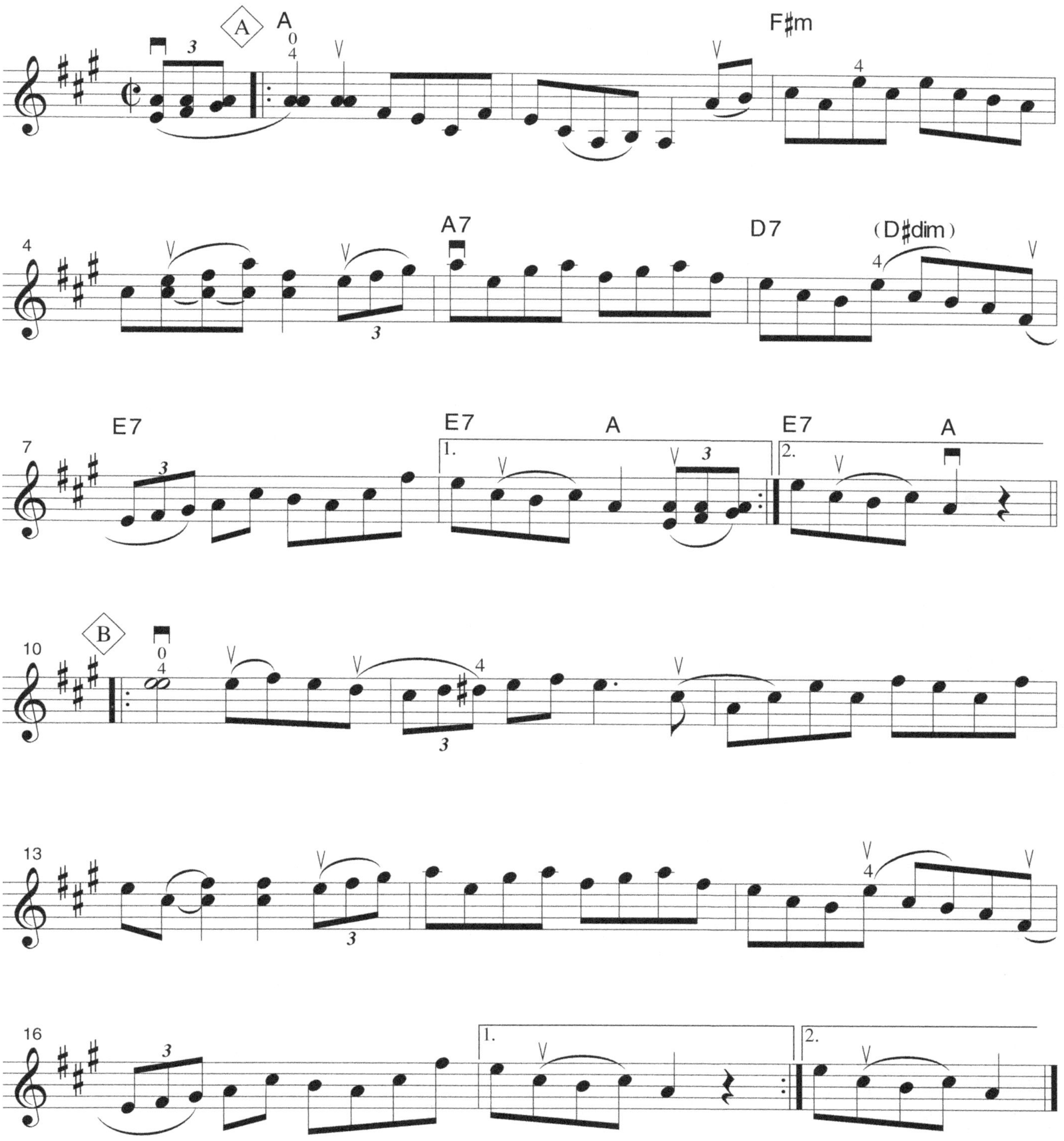

*In the style of Herman Johnson*

# Poor Girl's Waltz

Traditional

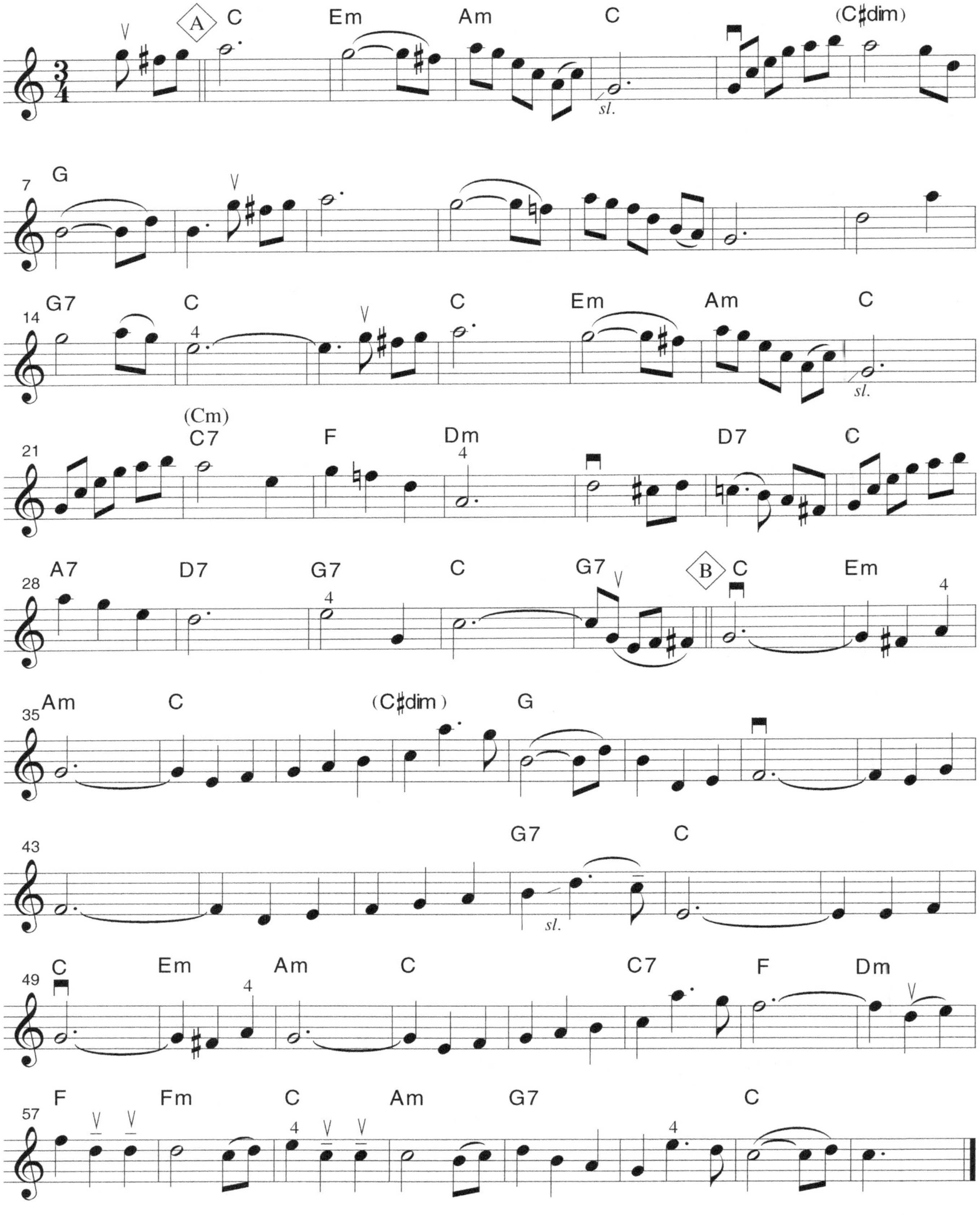

# Red Apple Rag

Swing Rhythm

Arthur Smith

*In the style of Herman Johnson*

© 1935 Glad Music/Pappy Daily Music. All rights reserved. Used with permission.

# Blue Eagle

Swing Rhythm

Traditional

*In the style of Herman Johnson*

# Molly Bloom

This tune was written by banjo player Alan Munde and is on a recording called "Poor Richard's Almanac" with Alan Munde and Sam Bush. It is a great tune to play on the fiddle.

Swing Rhythm

Alan Munde

*In the style of Herman Johnson*

© 1976, Kentucky Colonel Music. All rights reserved. Used with permission.

# Fort Smith

Traditional

*In the style of Herman Johnson*

# Martha Campbell

Traditional

*In the style of Herman Johnson*

# Peacock Rag

This tune brings back a childhood memory of being at the National Oldtime Fiddle Contest in Weiser, Idaho. There are peacocks at a farm near the contest site and every time I heard them squack I would think of the "Peacock Rag."

Swing Rhythm

Arthur Smith

© 1941 Glad Music/Pappy Daily Music. All rights reserved. Used with permission.

TRACK 9

# Rickett's Hornpipe

Traditional

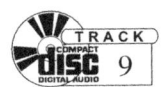

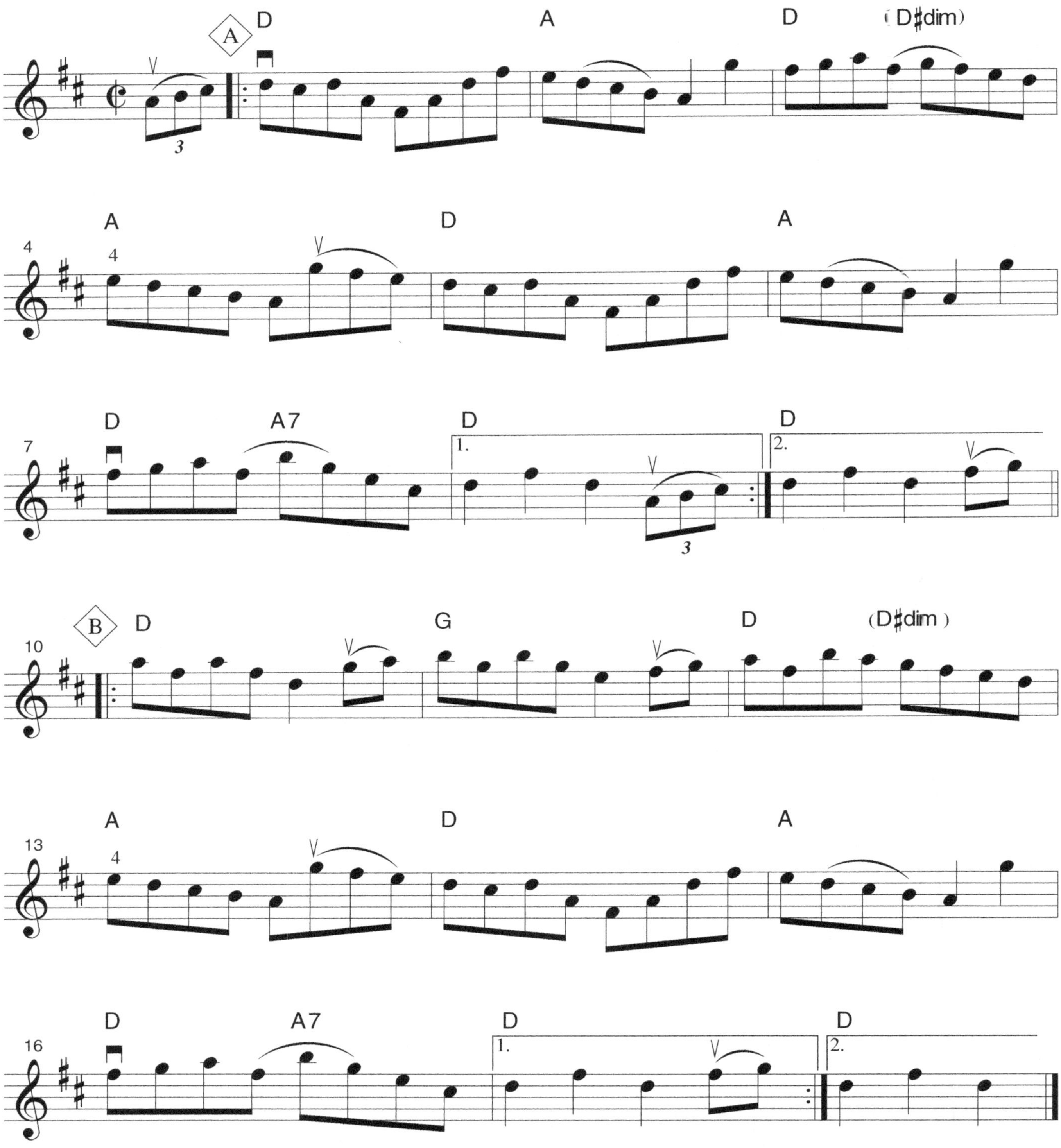


*In the style of Herman Johnson*

# Blackberry Blossom

This version presents the basic tune and then adds some variation.

Traditional

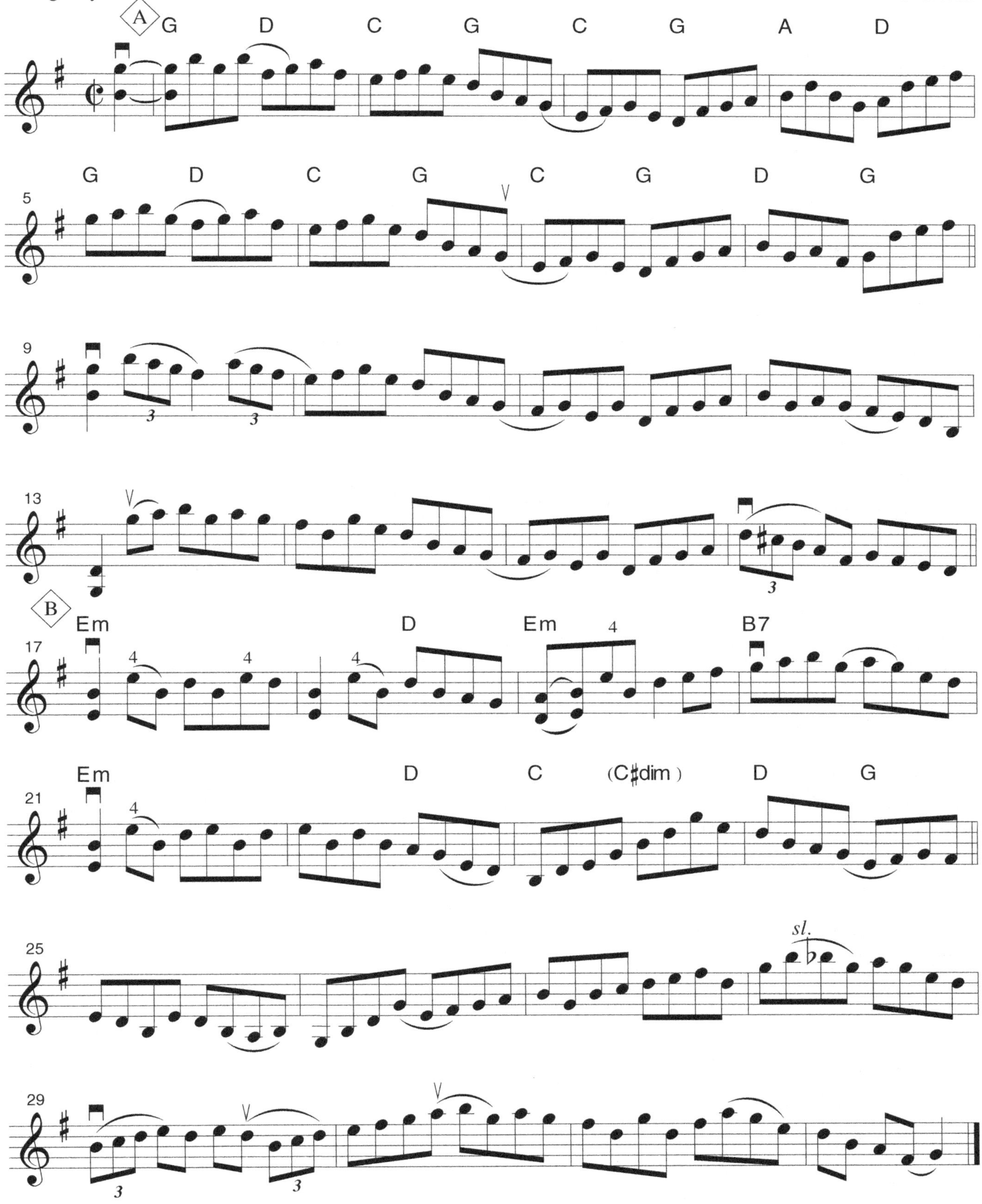

TRACK 11

# Here and There

This tune is similar to "Coming Down from Denver."

Traditional

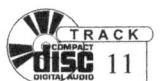

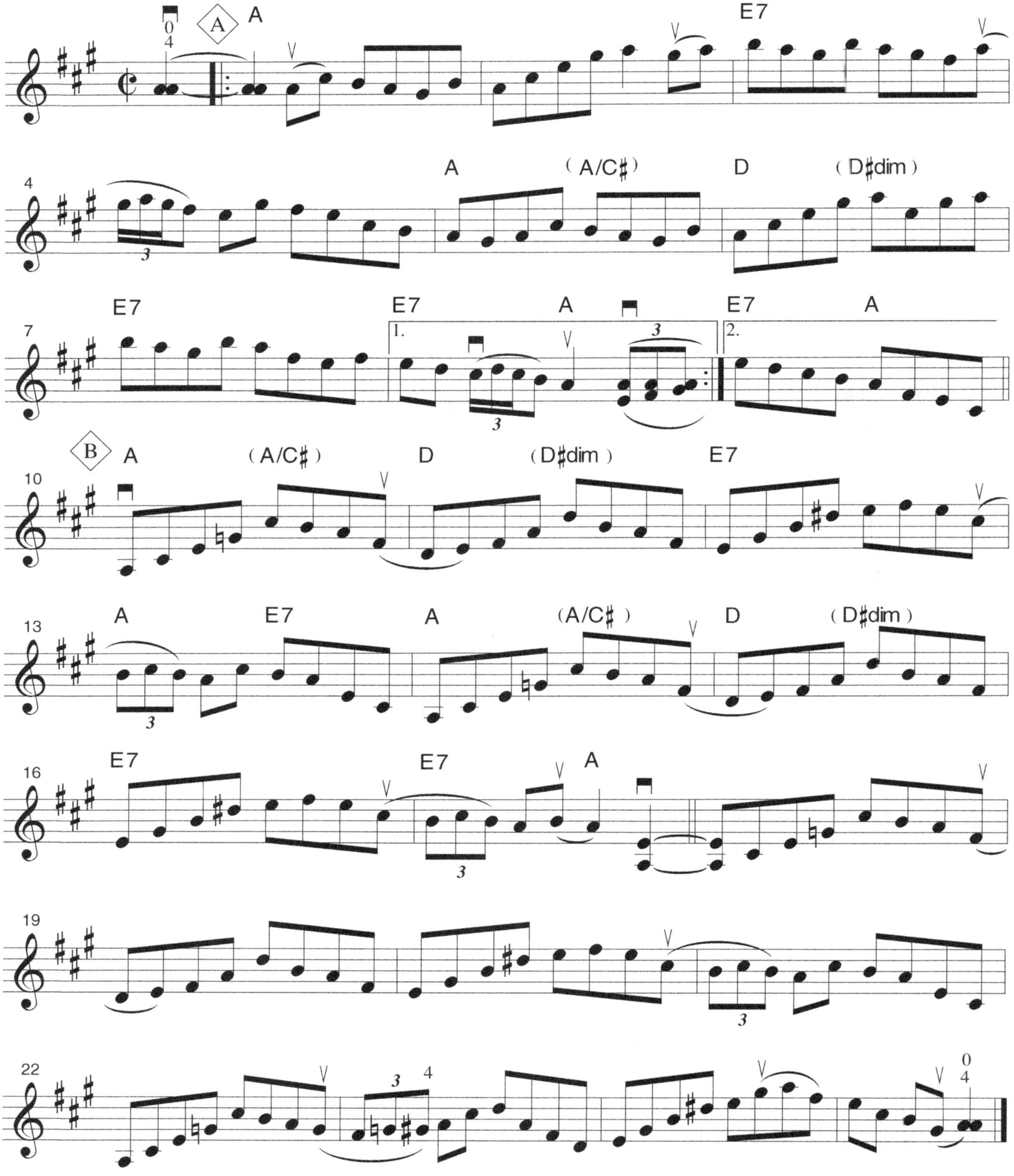


*In the style of Herman Johnson*

# Richmond Polka

This tune may also be known as "Old Aunt Sally There's a Bug on Me."

Traditional

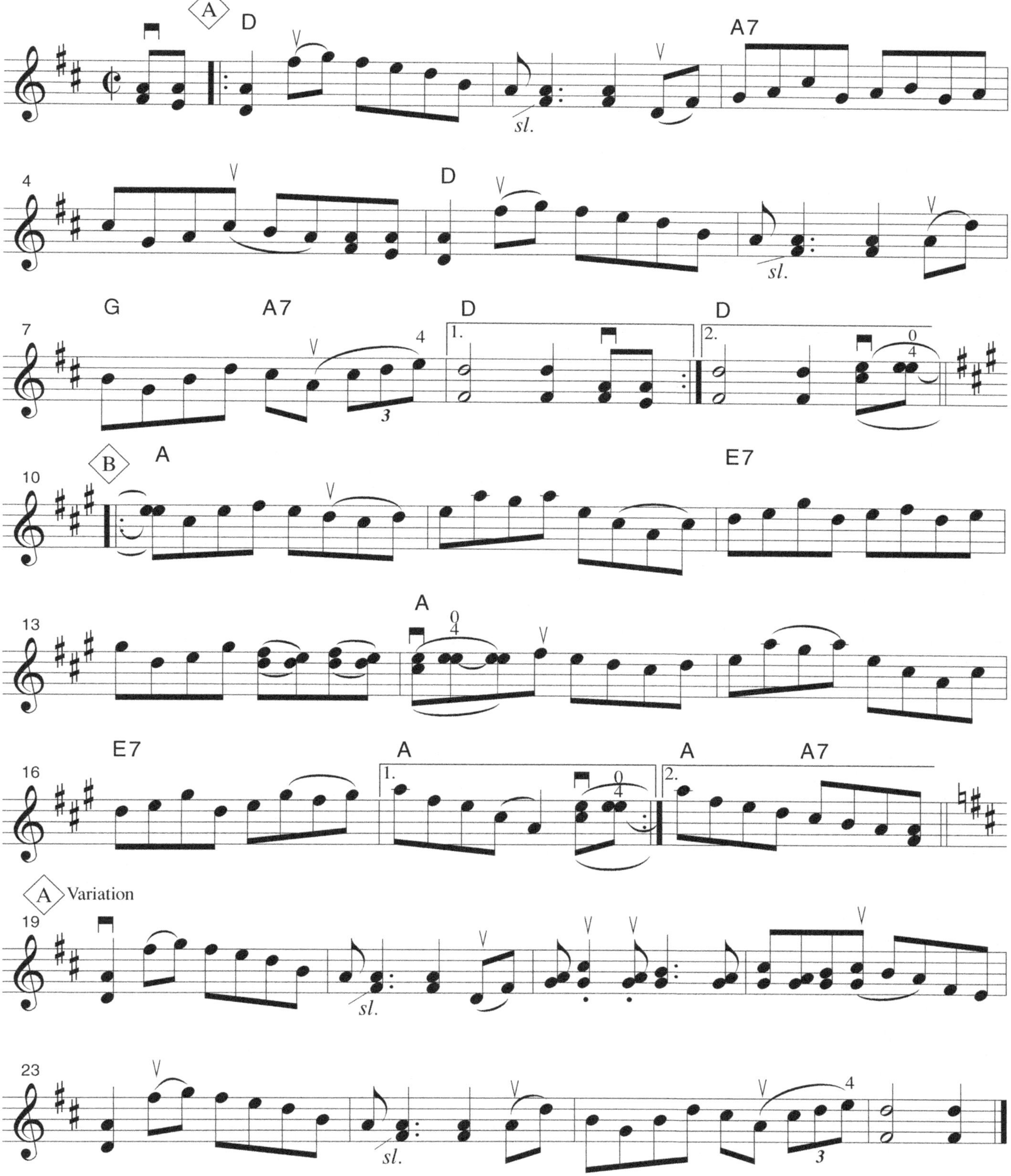

*In the style of Herman Johnson*

# Old Sport

*Traditional*

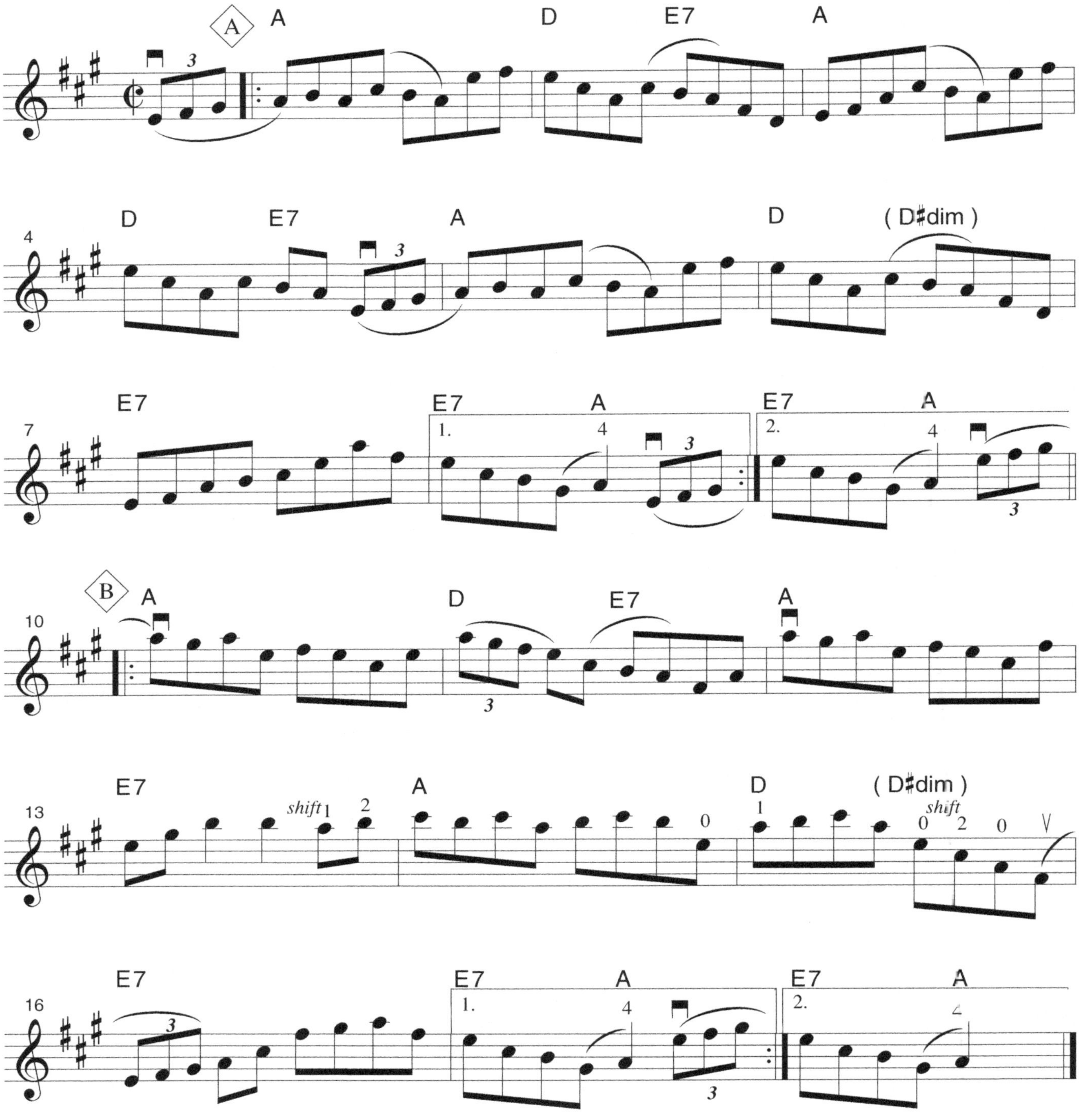

*In the style of Herman Johnson*

# Fiddler's Dream

Traditional

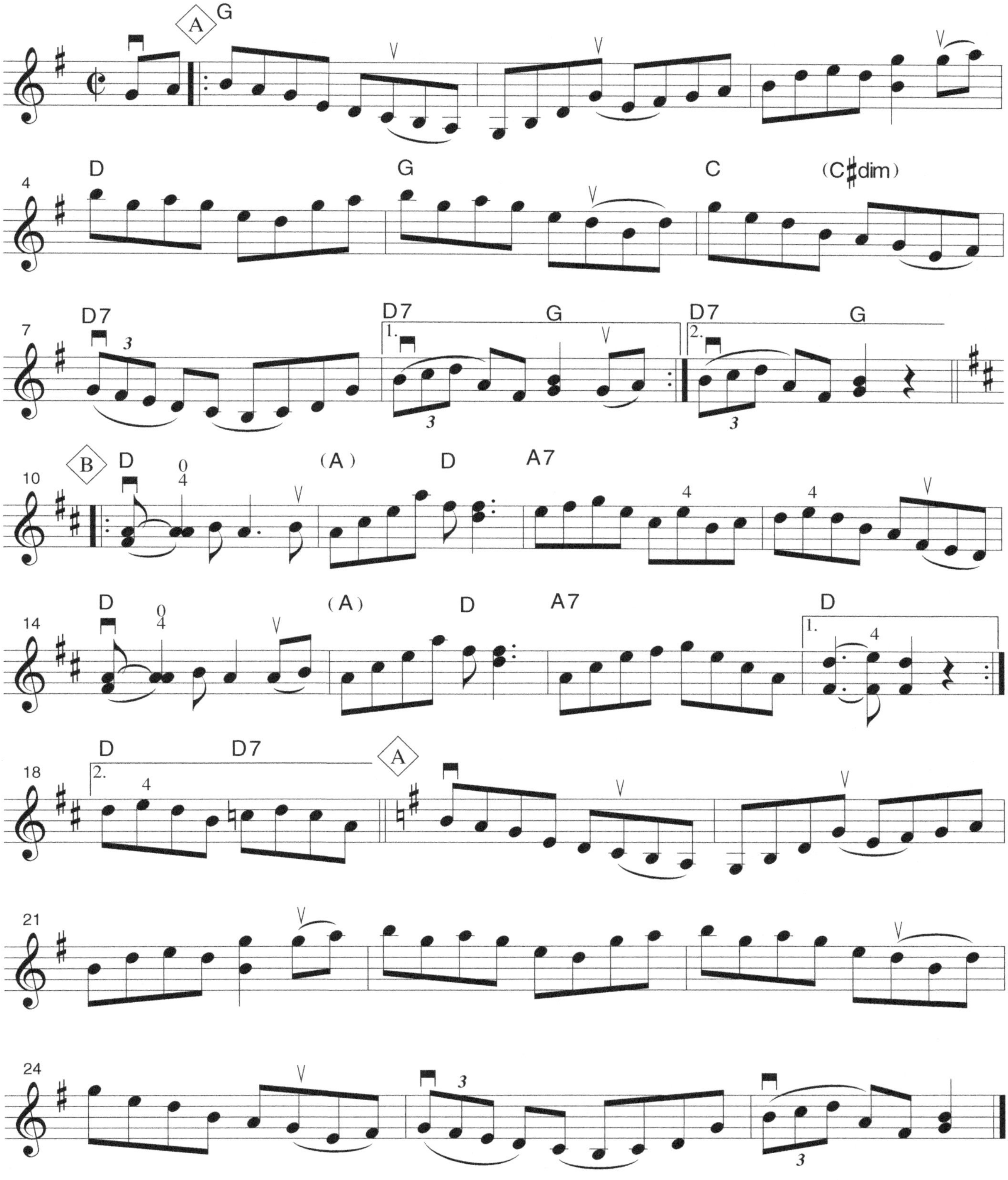

*In the style of Herman Johnson*

TRACK 15

# Paddy on the Turnpike

Traditional

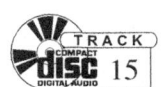

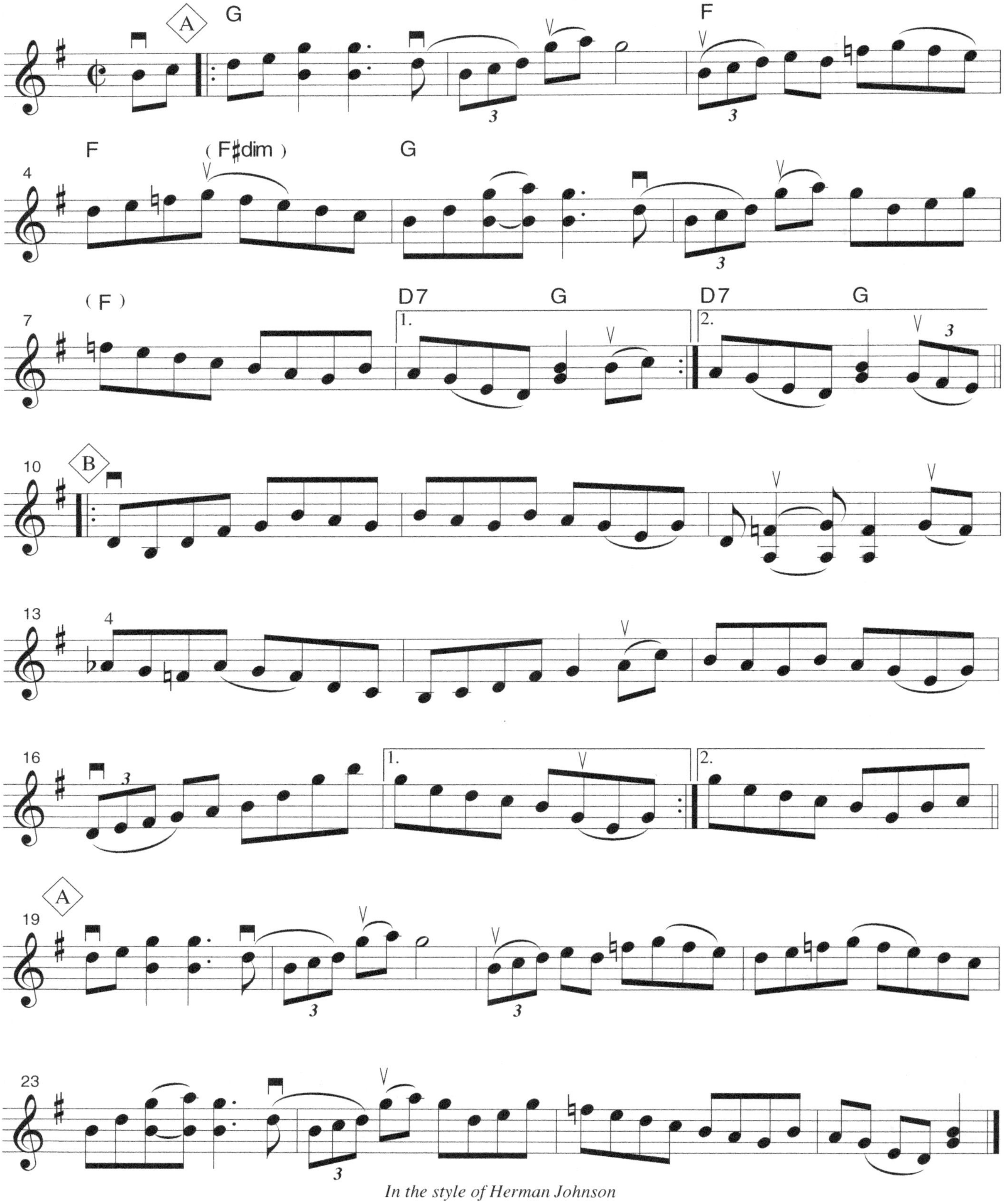


*In the style of Herman Johnson*

# Georgiana Moon

Traditional

Swing Rhythm
(on eighth notes)

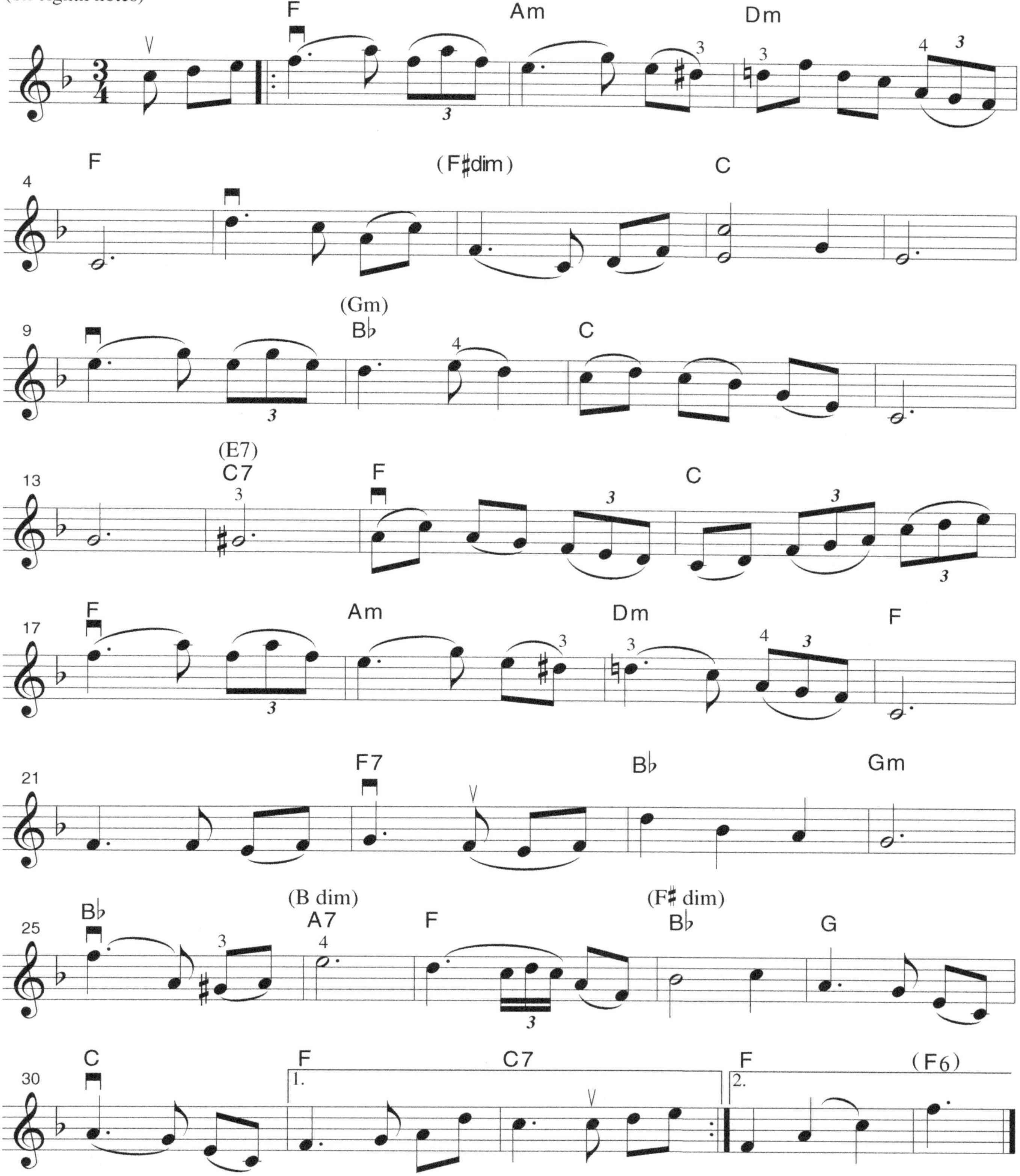

# Fisher's Hornpipe

This version has a third part added which has become popular among fiddlers.

Traditional

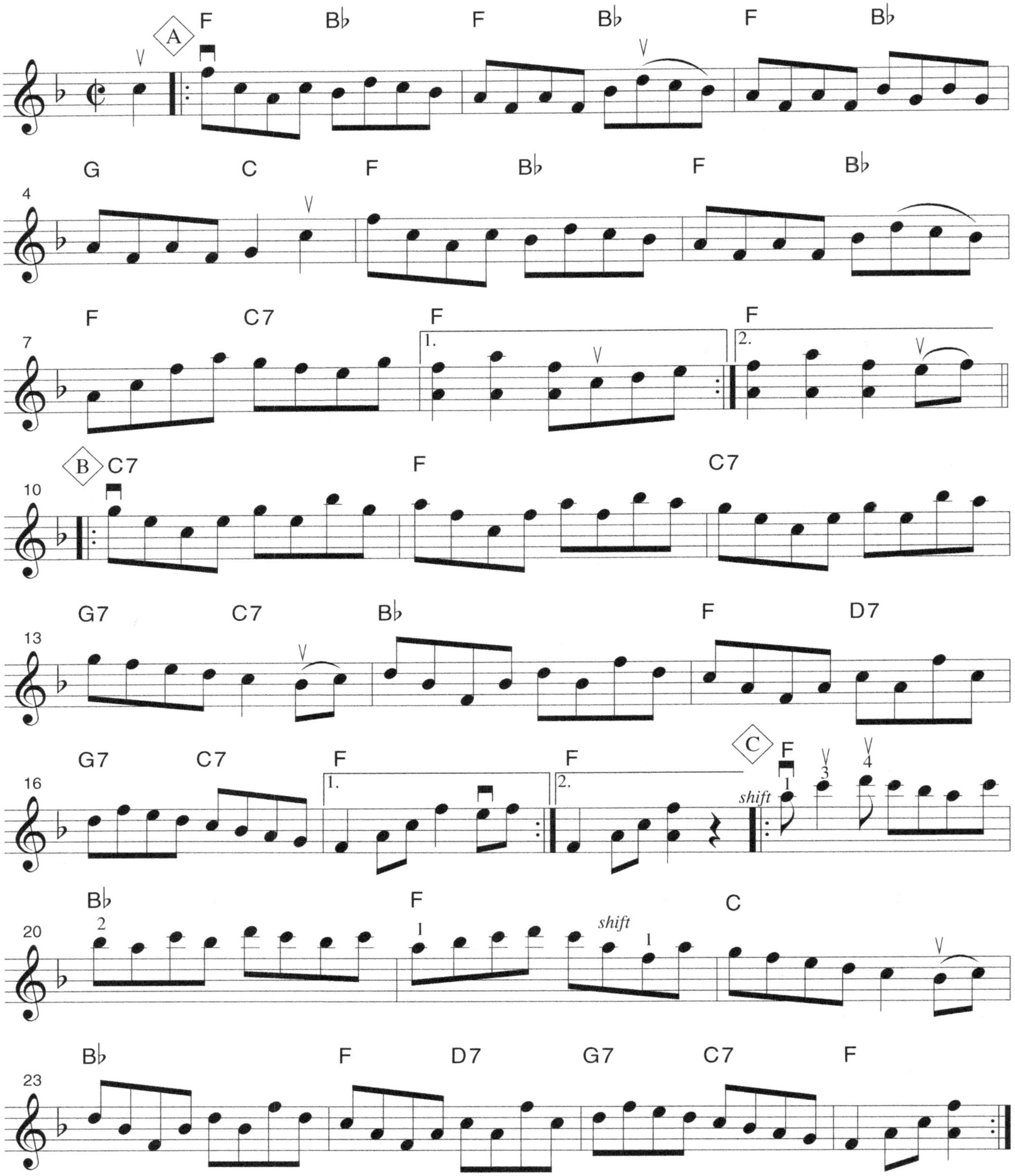

# Pacific Slope

Traditional

*Reach 4th finger up 1 step.

*In the style of Herman Johnson*

# Cincinnati Rag

# Bill Cheatum

*Swing Rhythm*                                  Traditional

*In the style of Herman Johnson*

TRACK 21

# Hot Foot

Swing Rhythm

Traditional

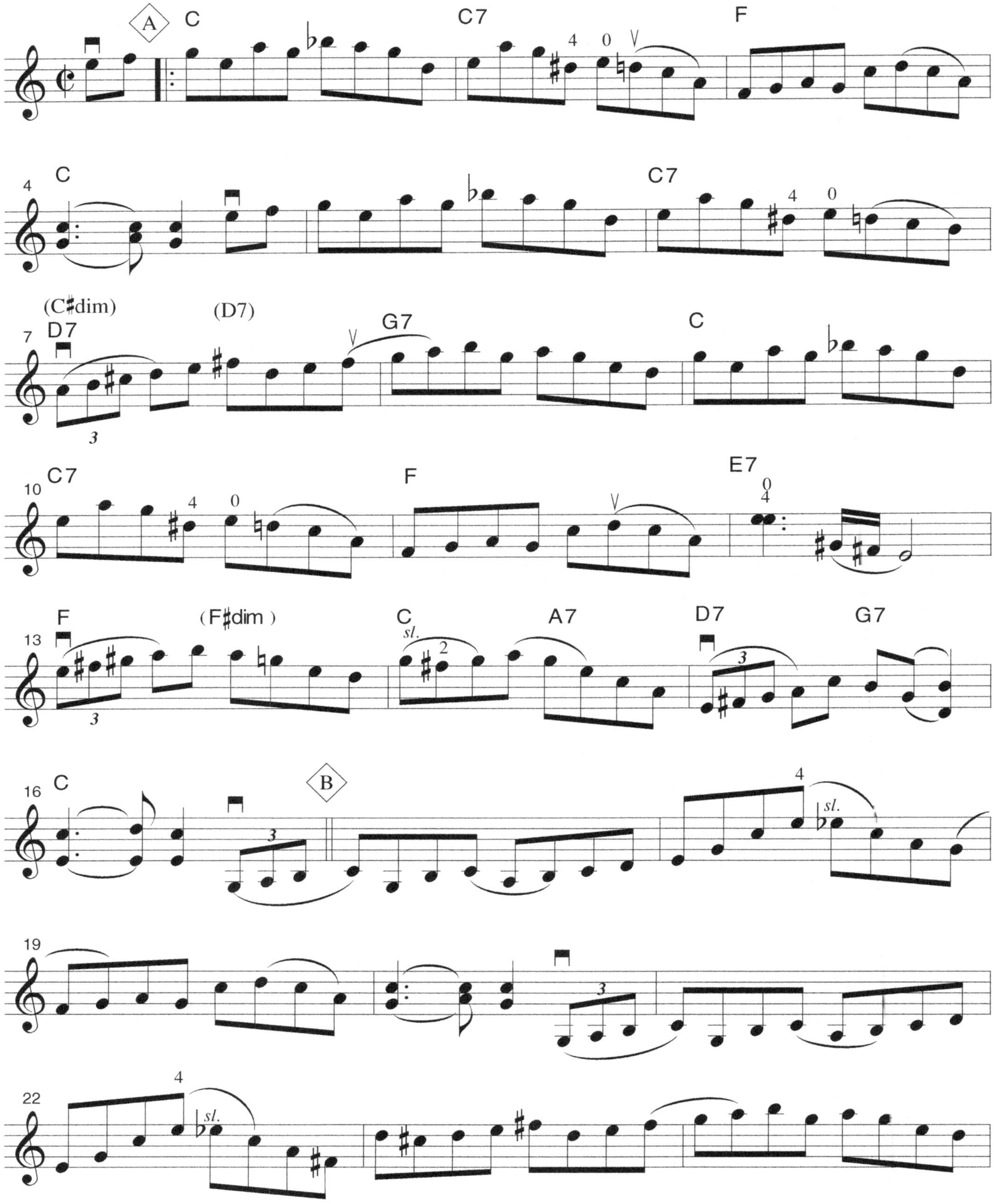

*In the style of Herman Johnson*

# Westphalia Waltz

Many fiddlers play this tune in the key of G. I first
learned it in the key of A as it is presented in this version.

Traditional

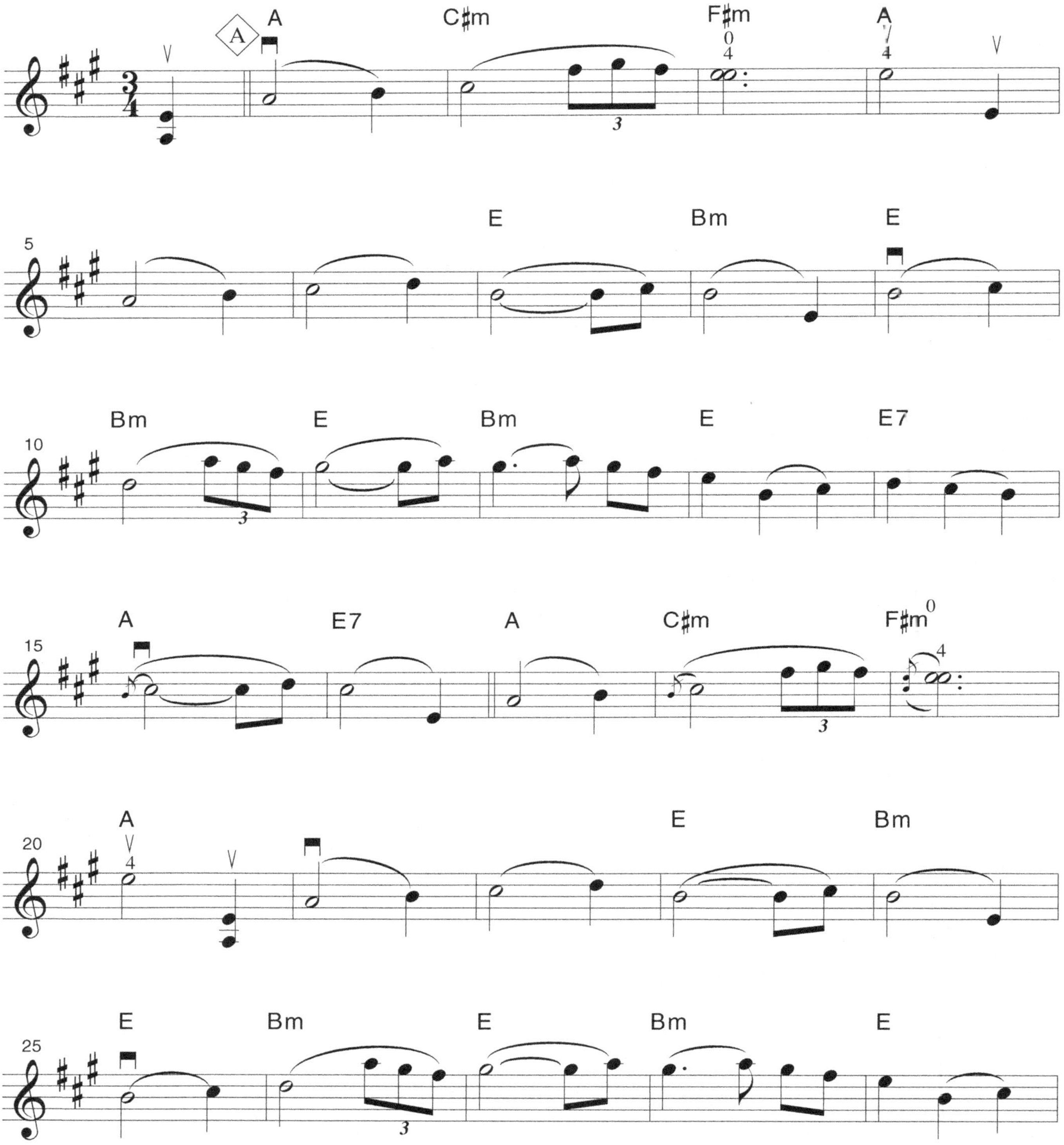

TRACK 23

# Hot Springs

This tune is said to have been written by Oklahoma fiddler, Orville Burns.

Swing Rhythm

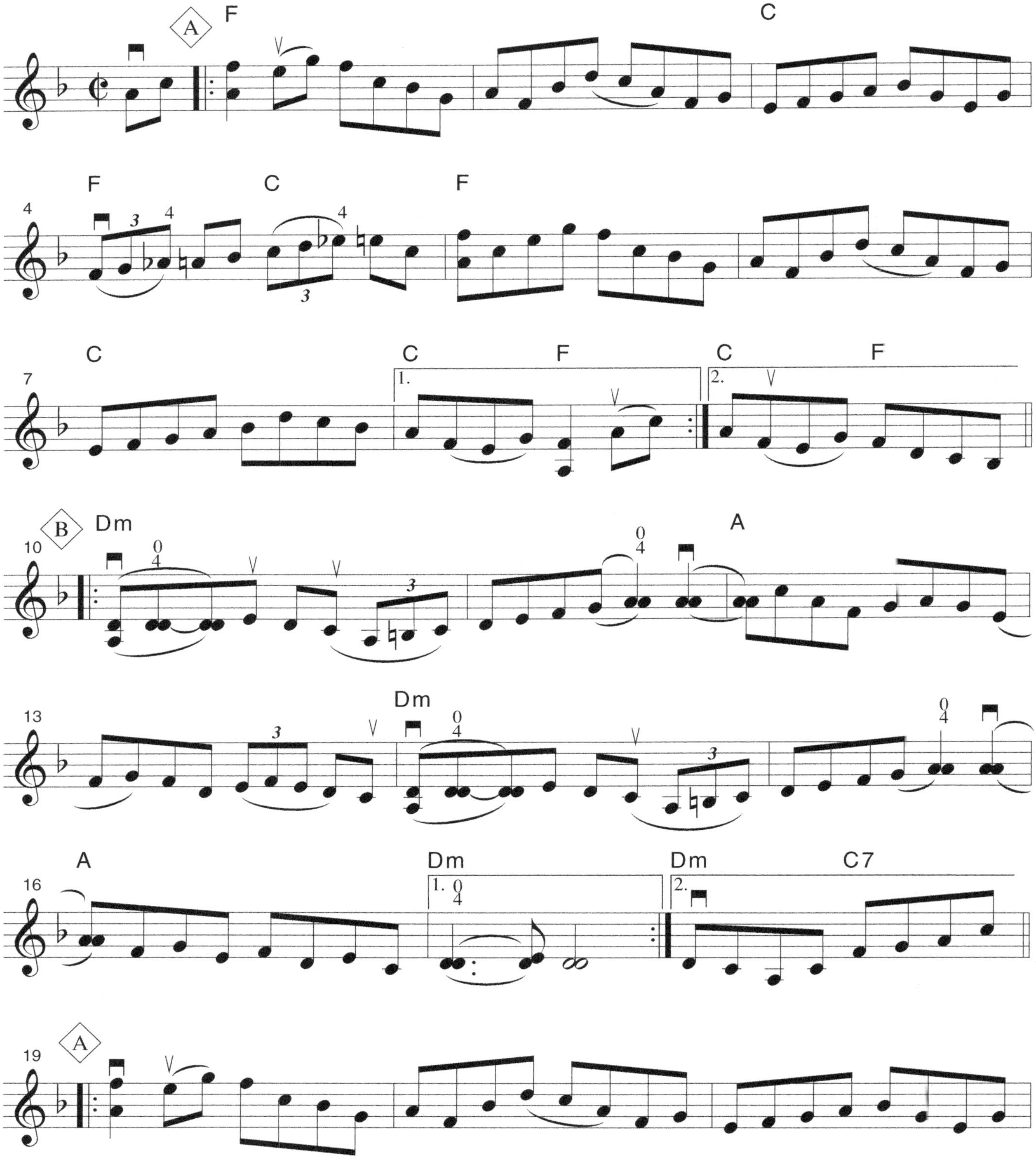

*In the style of Herman Johnson*

# George Booker

Traditional

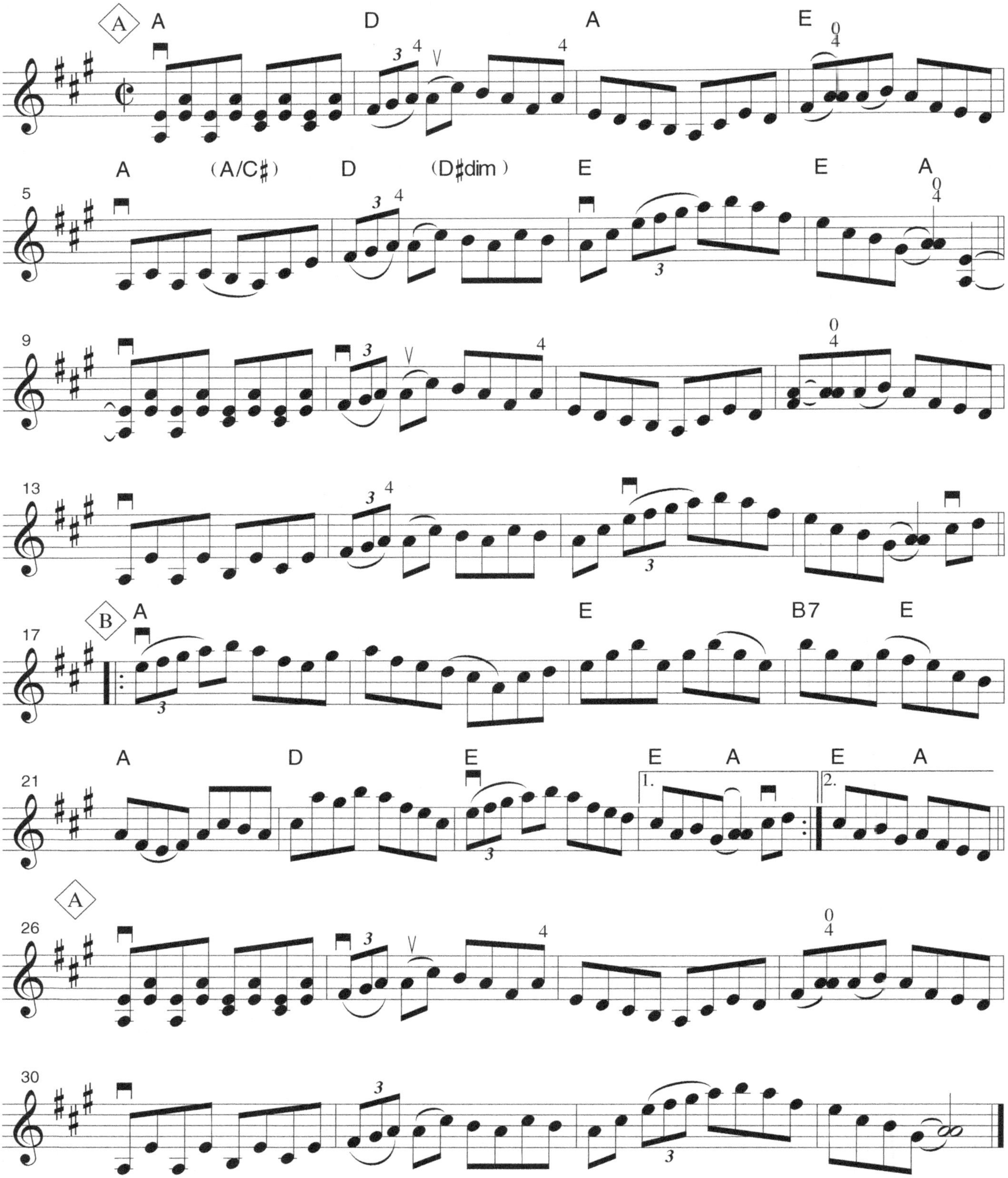

*In the style of Herman Johnson*

# Little Betty Brown

*Swing Rhythm*

Traditional

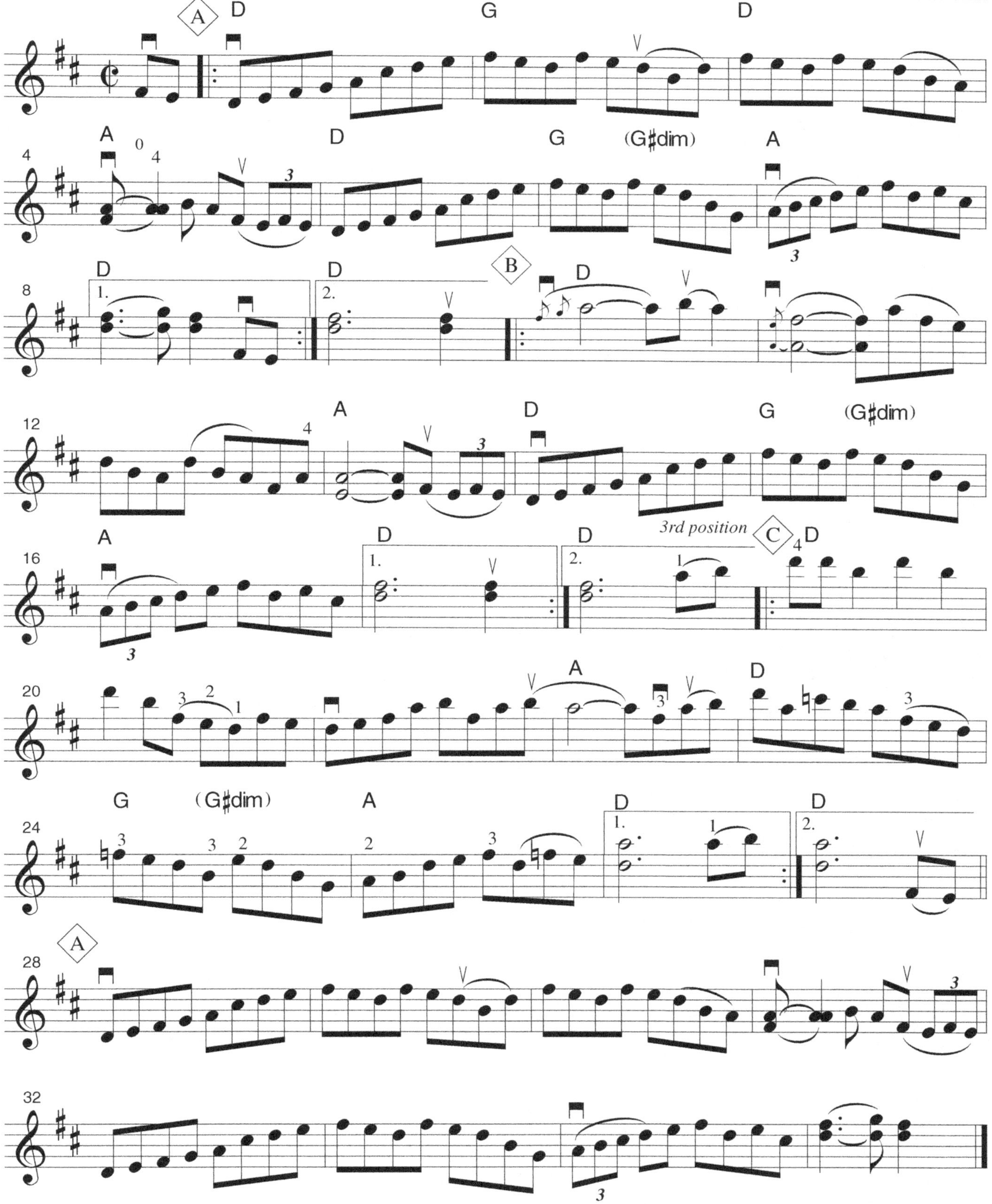

*In the style of Herman Johnson*

# Ostinello Reel

This tune is good to practice shifting. Be sure to reach extra high to get the high E in tune.

Traditional

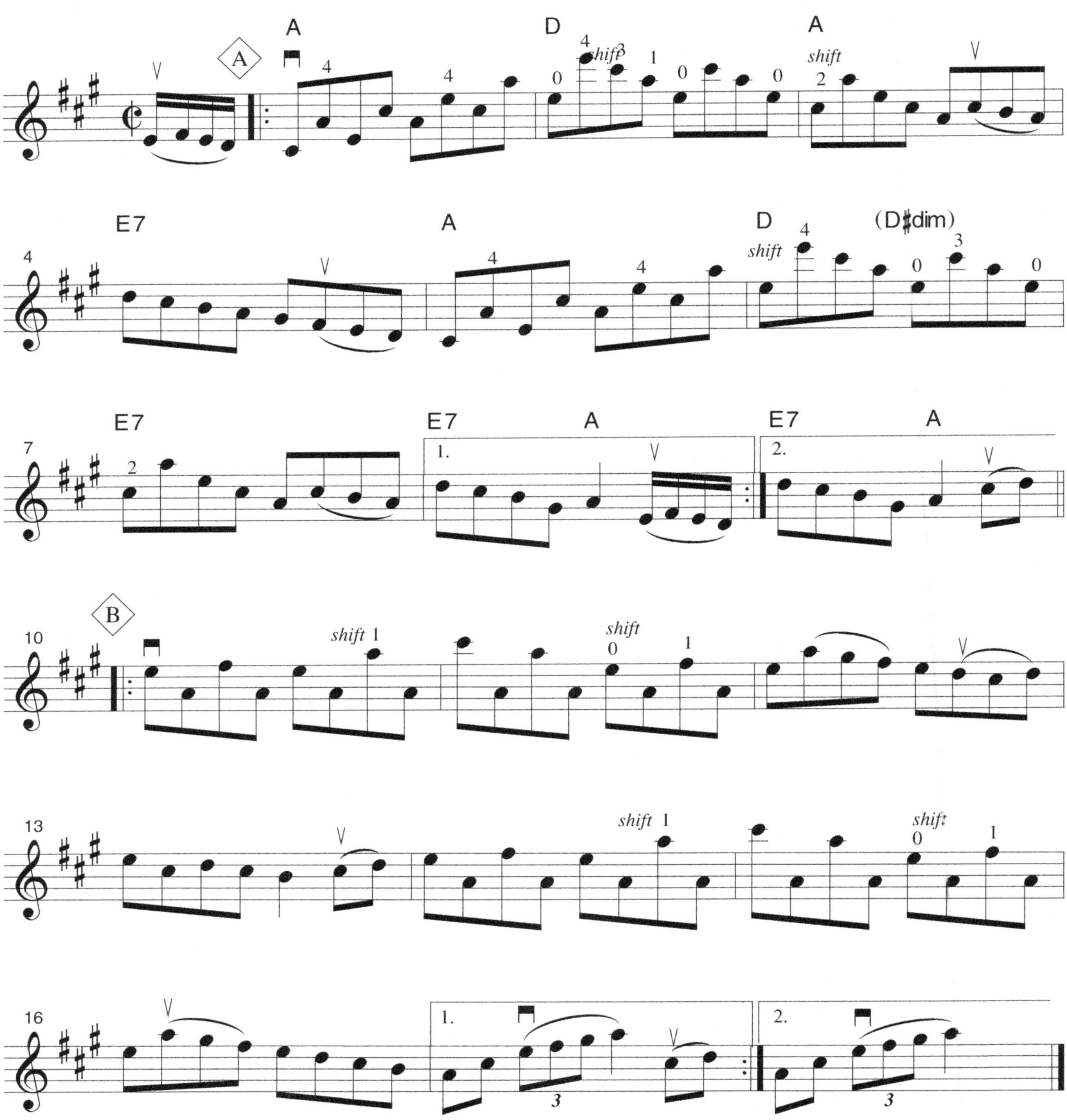

*In the style of Herman Johnson*

# Miller's Reel

This version is based on the playing of Andy Emert.
Written by Zeke Backus.

Traditional

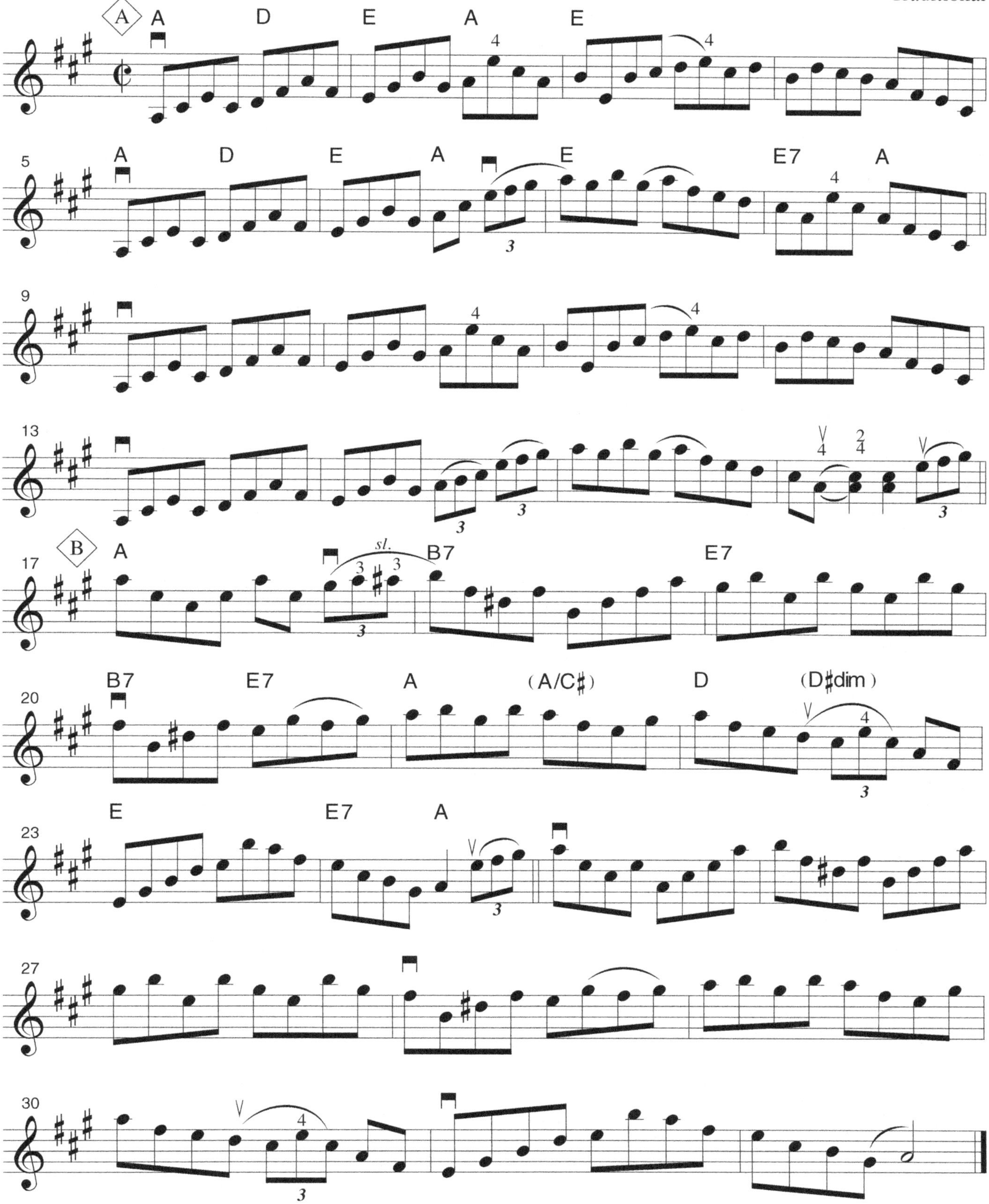

*In the style of Andy Emert*

# Cabri Waltz

*Cabri Waltz* is presented in two different versions. The first is the basic melody and the second is a more advanced version which is based on the playing of Herman Johnson. Emphasize a swing rhythm on the eighth notes.

Traditional

Swing Rhythm

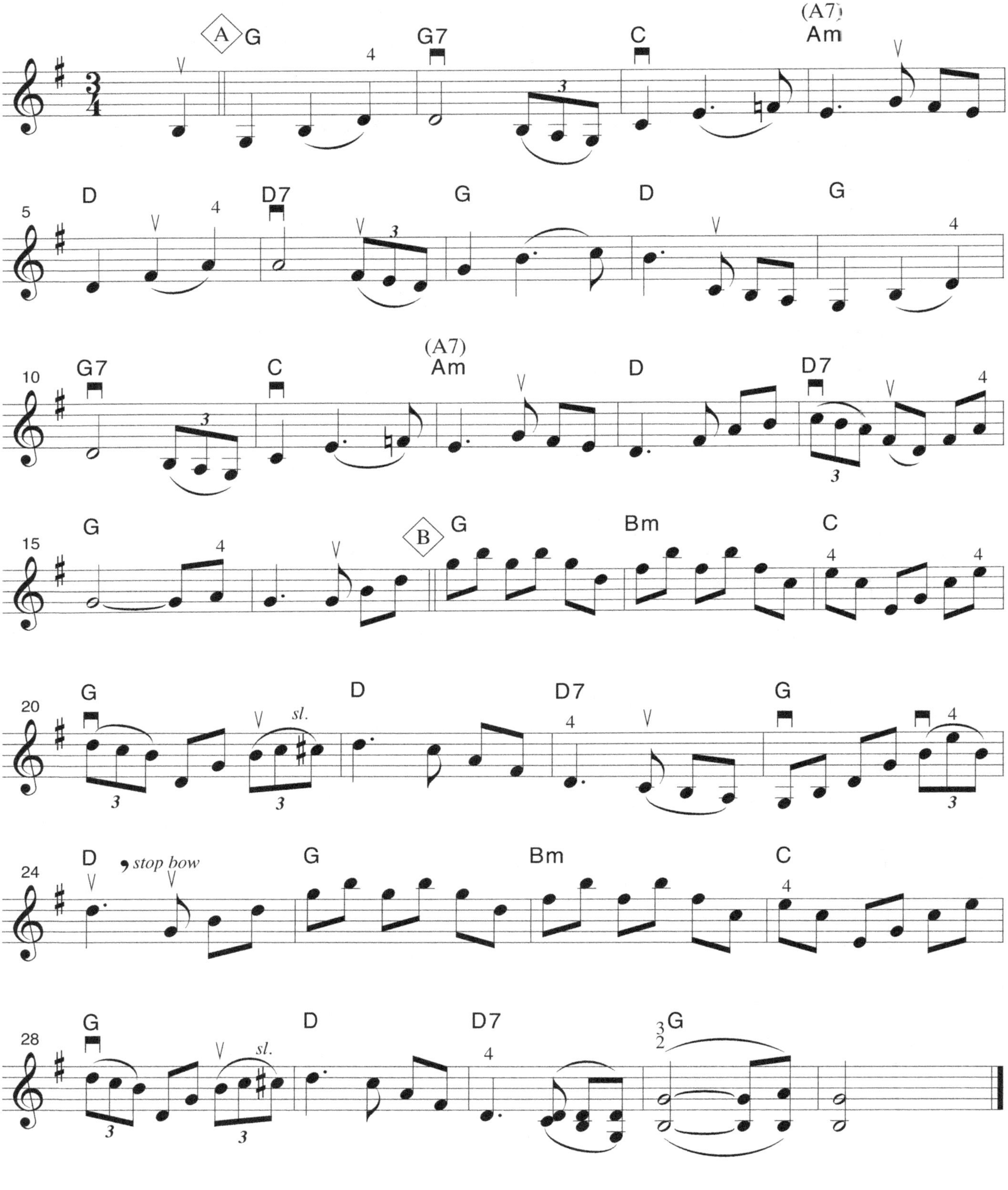

In the style of Herman Johnson

# Choctaw

Swing Rhythm

Traditional

*In the style of Herman Johnson*

# Indian See-Saw

This unusual tune is also known as "Hell Amongst the Moonshiners."

Traditional

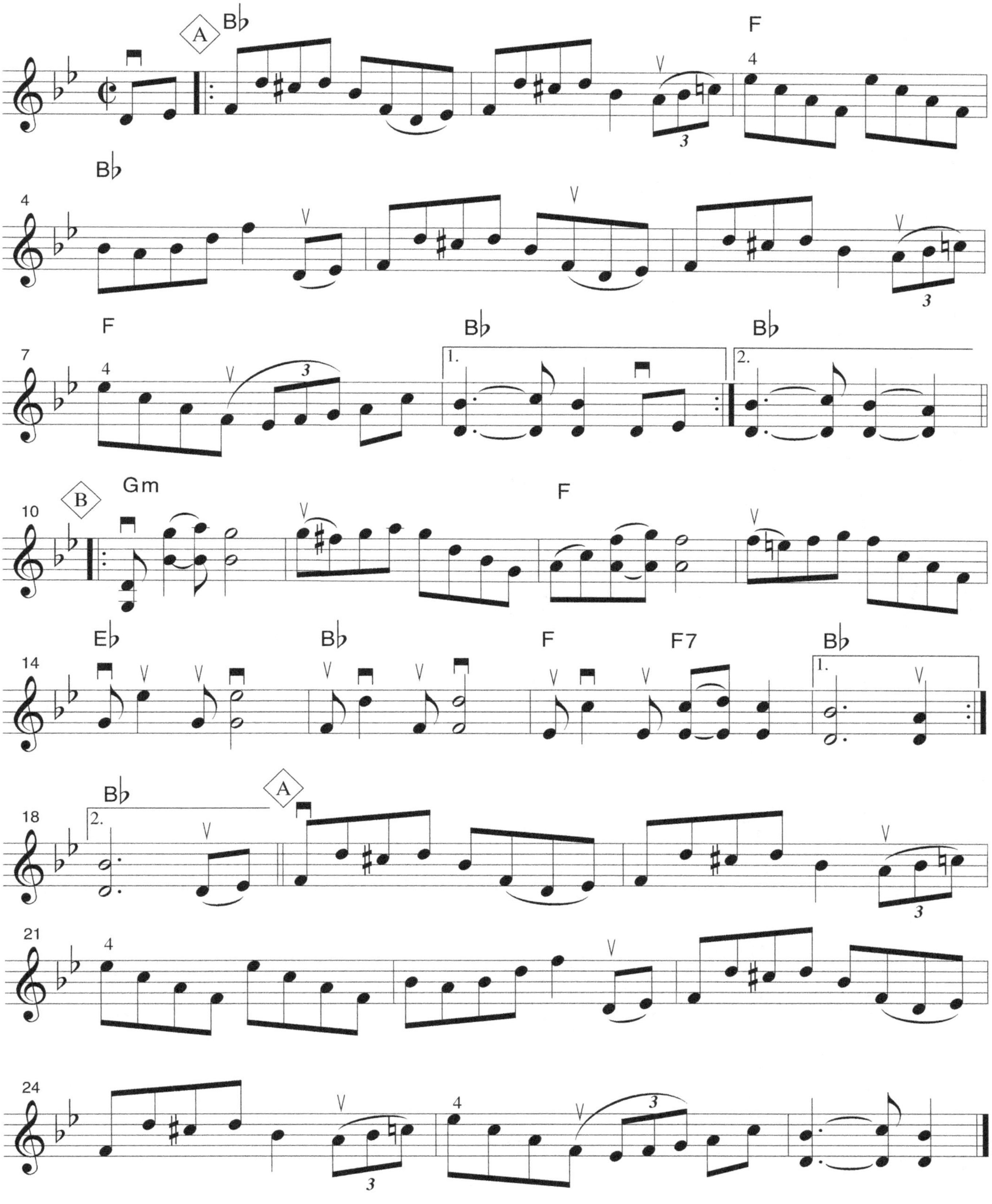

# Coming Down From Denver

This version is based on the playing of Byron Berline and Dick Barrett.

Traditional

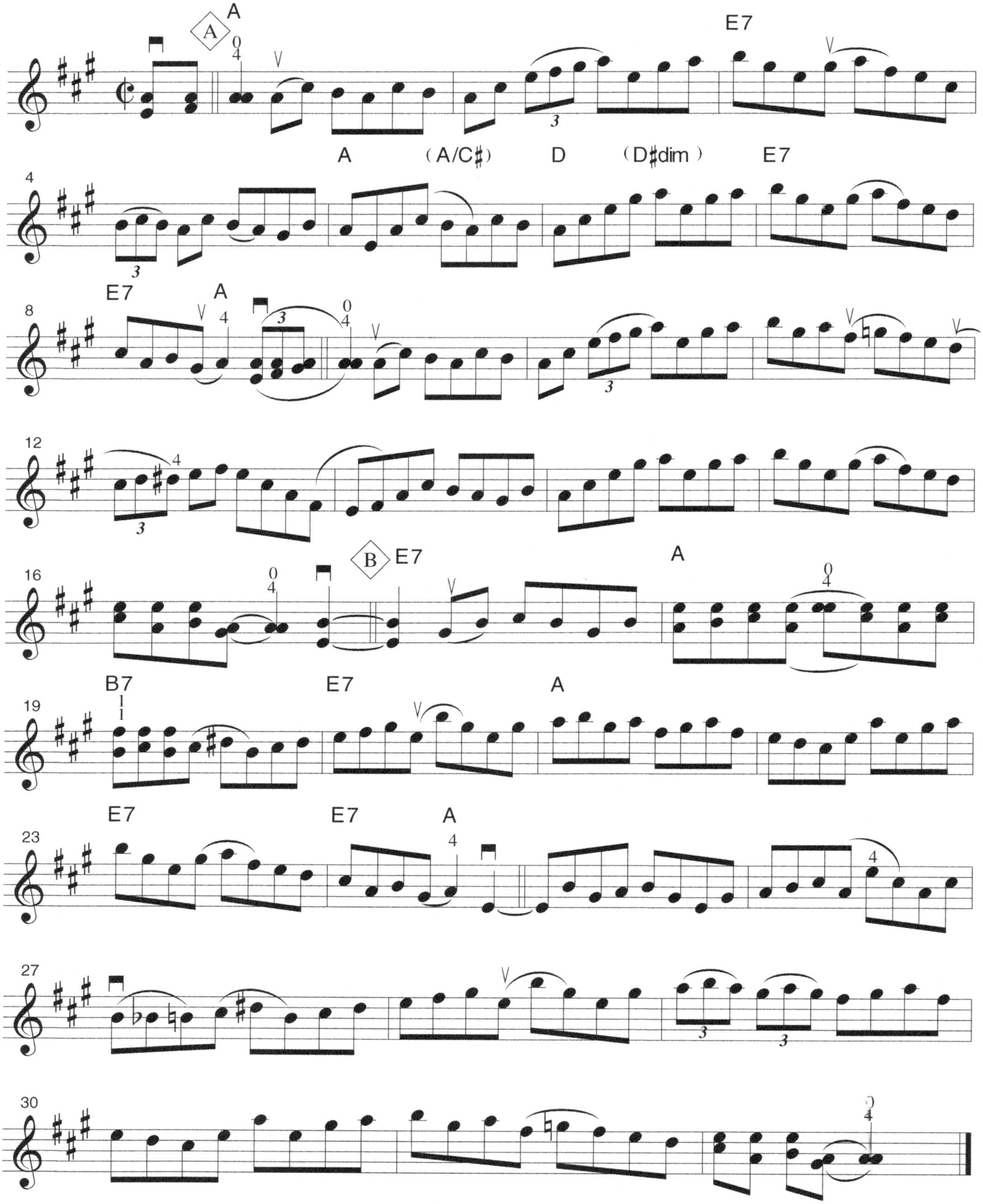

# Wagoner Hornpipe

*Traditional*

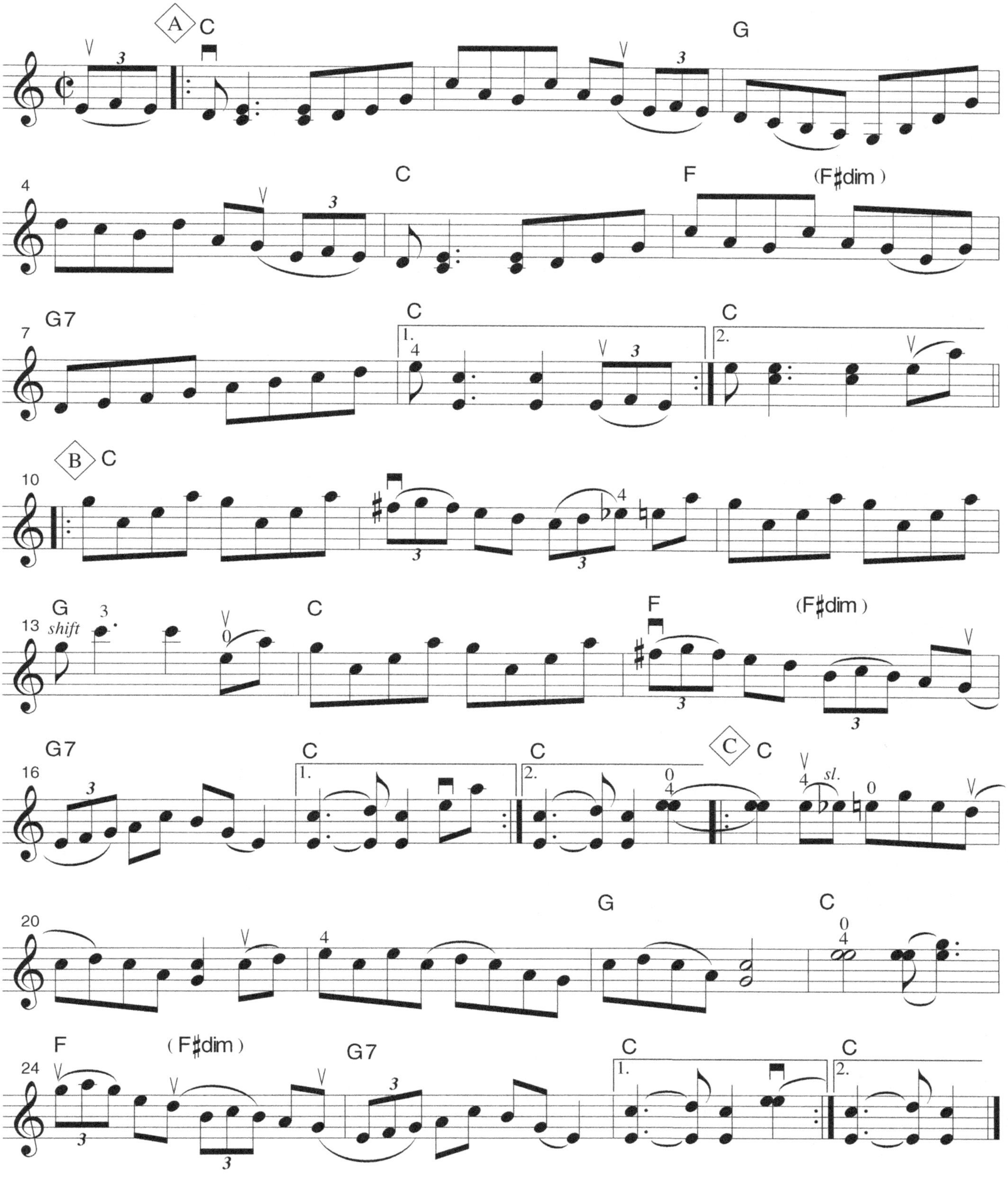

*In the style of Herman Johnson*

# Smith's Reel

The Ⓒ section of this song is not part of the original song but it has become popular among fiddlers.

Traditional

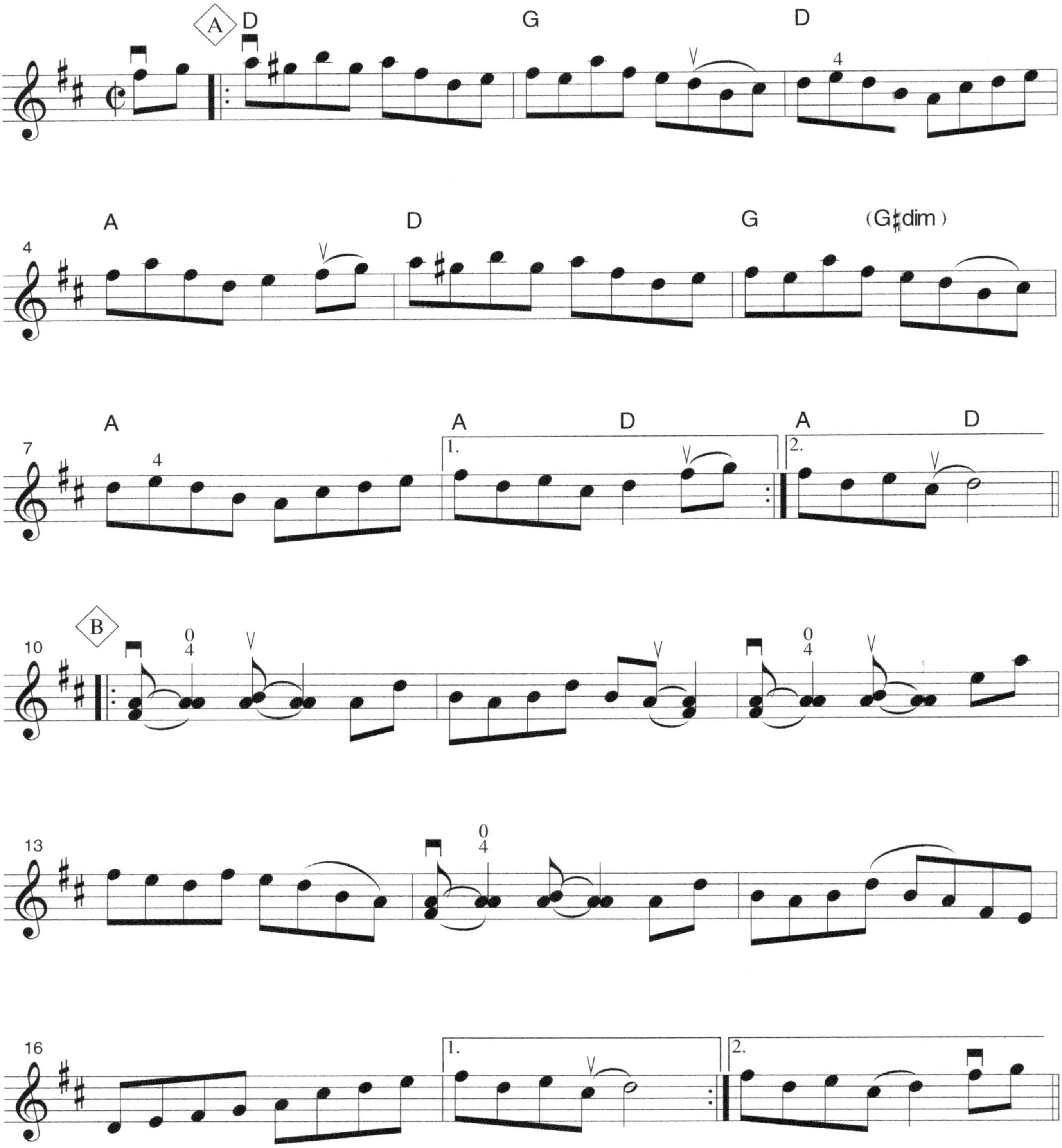

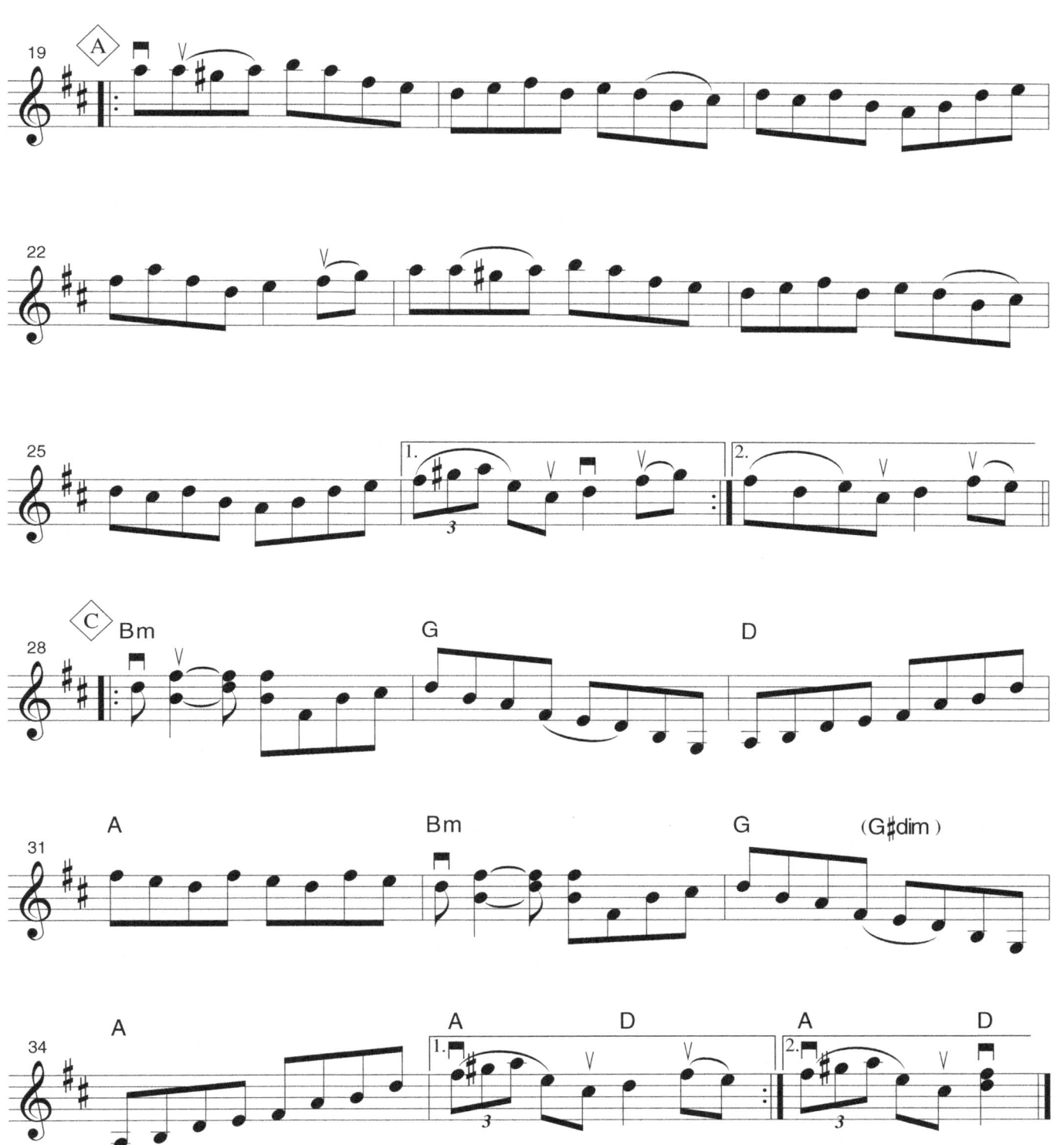

*In the style of Herman Johnson*

TRACK 34

# Sixteen Days in Georgia

This tune may also be known as *Fourteen Days in Georgia*.
The first section has an extra measure making nine bars.

Swing Rhythm

Traditional

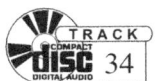

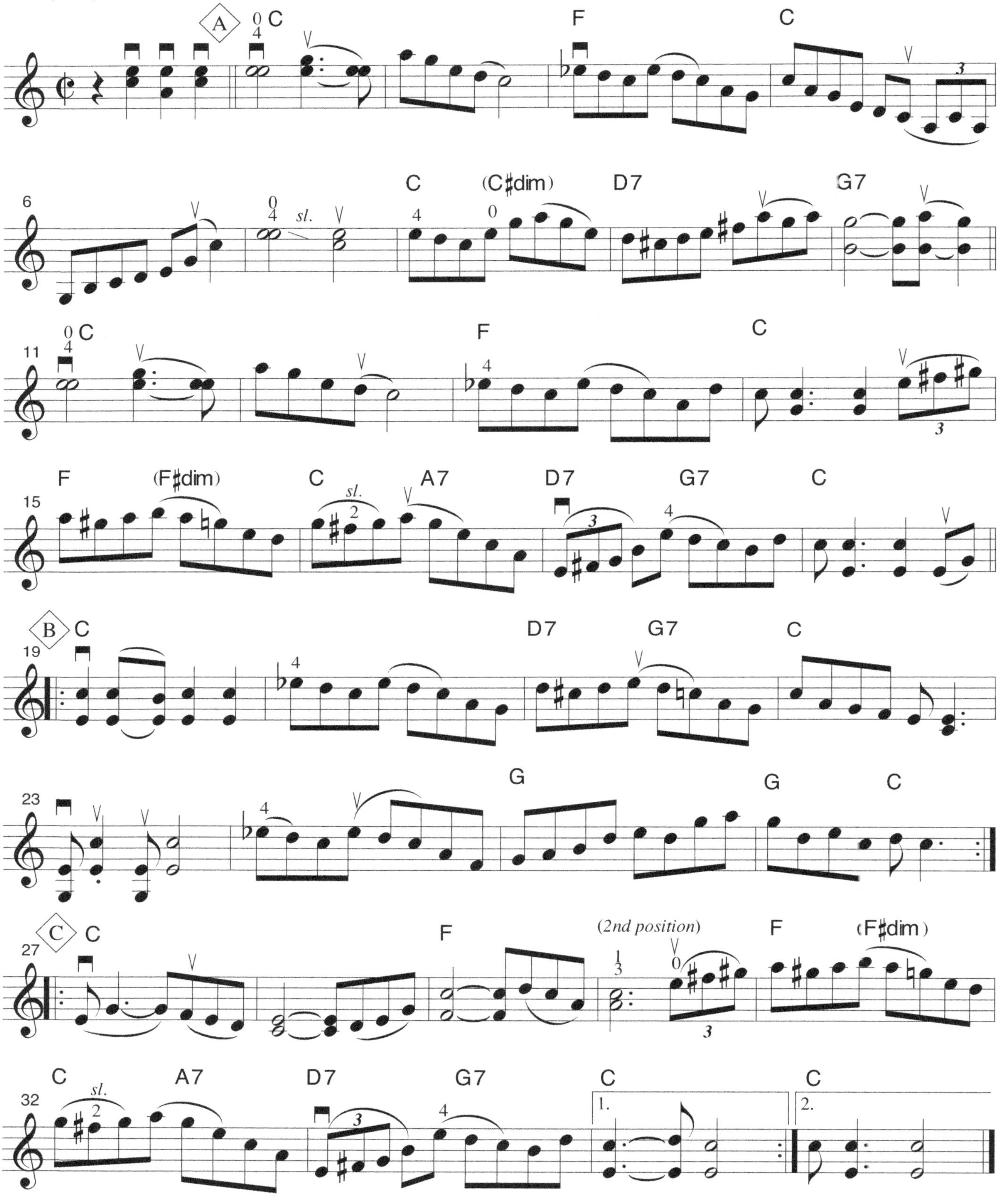


*In the style of Herman Johnson*

# Redbird Hornpipe

Traditional

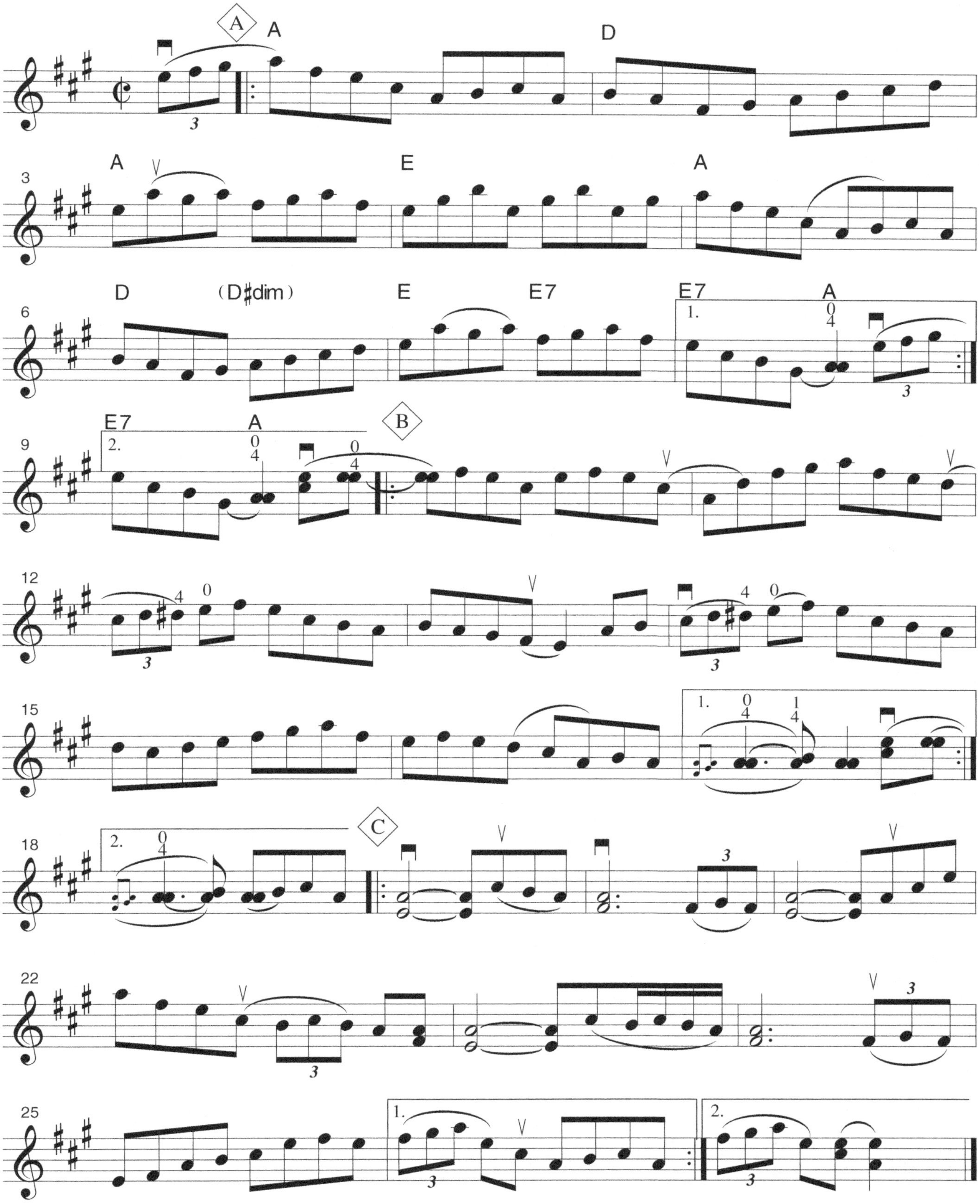

*In the style of Herman Johnson*

# I Don't Love Nobody

This tune is often played in the key of A. This version is in C and Am.

Swing Rhythm

Traditional

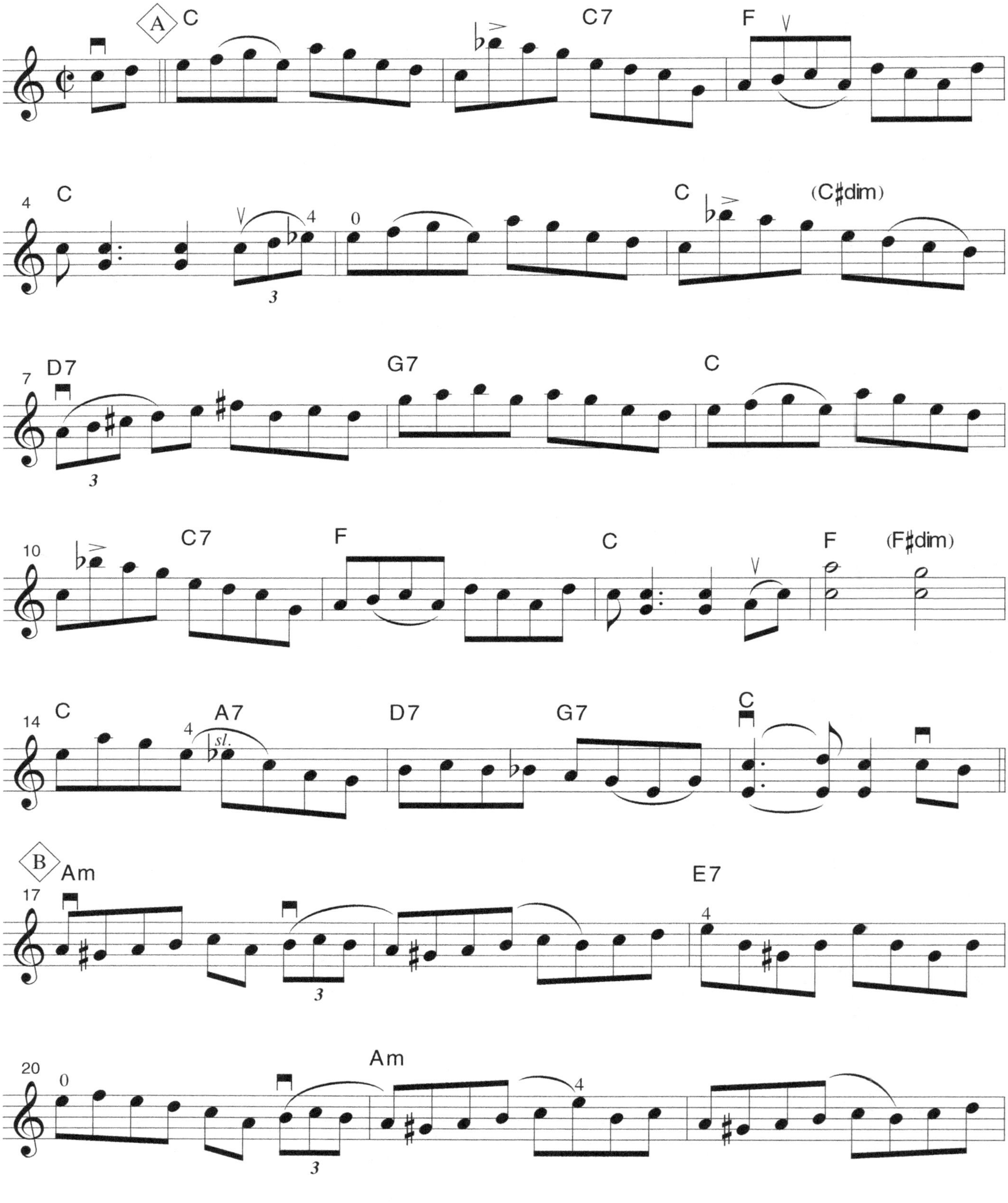

In the style of Herman Johnson

# Sally Ann

Traditional

*Reach 4th finger up 1 step

*In the style of Herman Johnson*

# Shortnin' Bread

Swing Rhythm  
Traditional

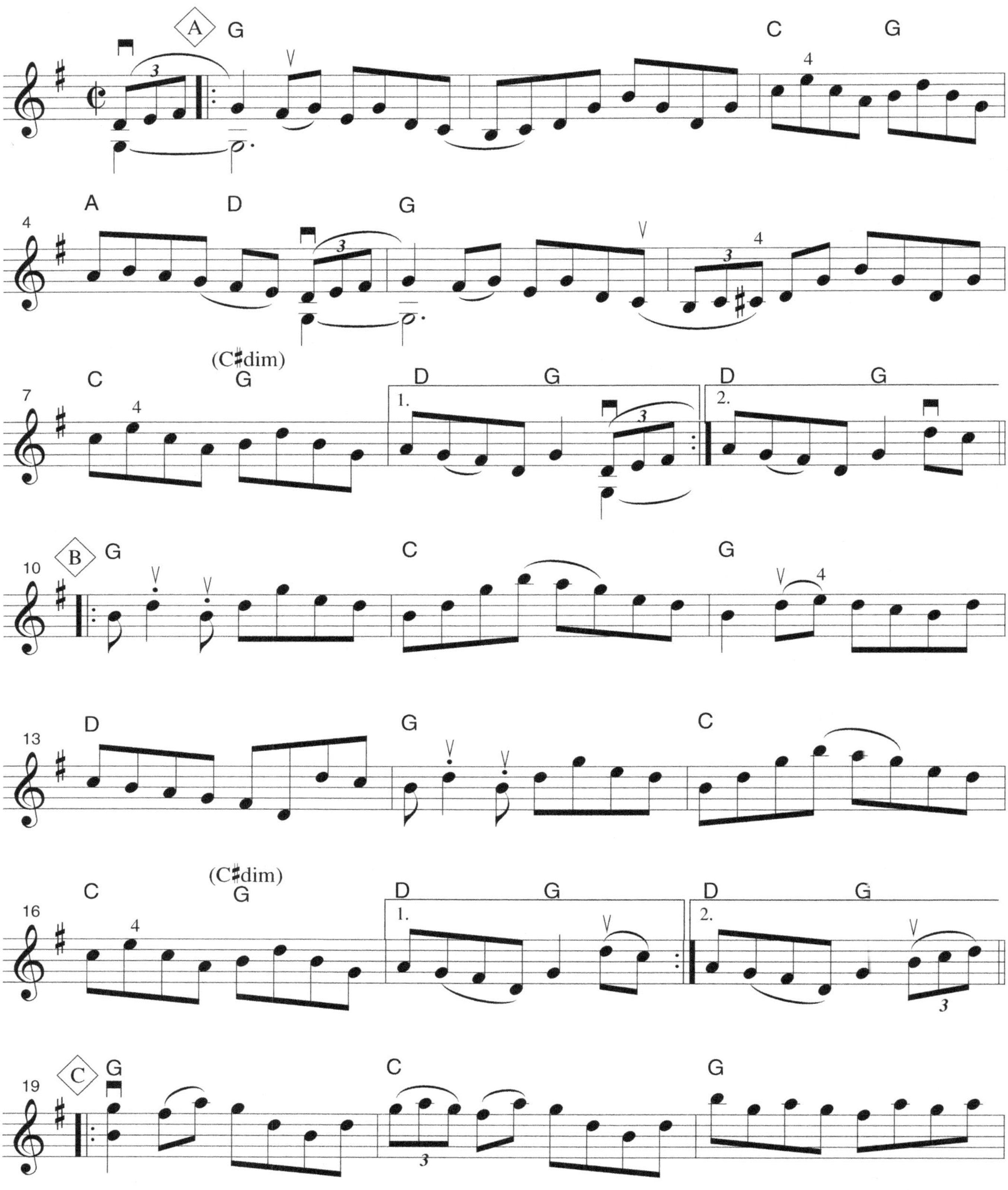

*In the style of Herman Johnson*

# Beaumont Rag

*This version is based on the playing of Loretta Brank.*

Swing Rhythm                                                                 Traditional

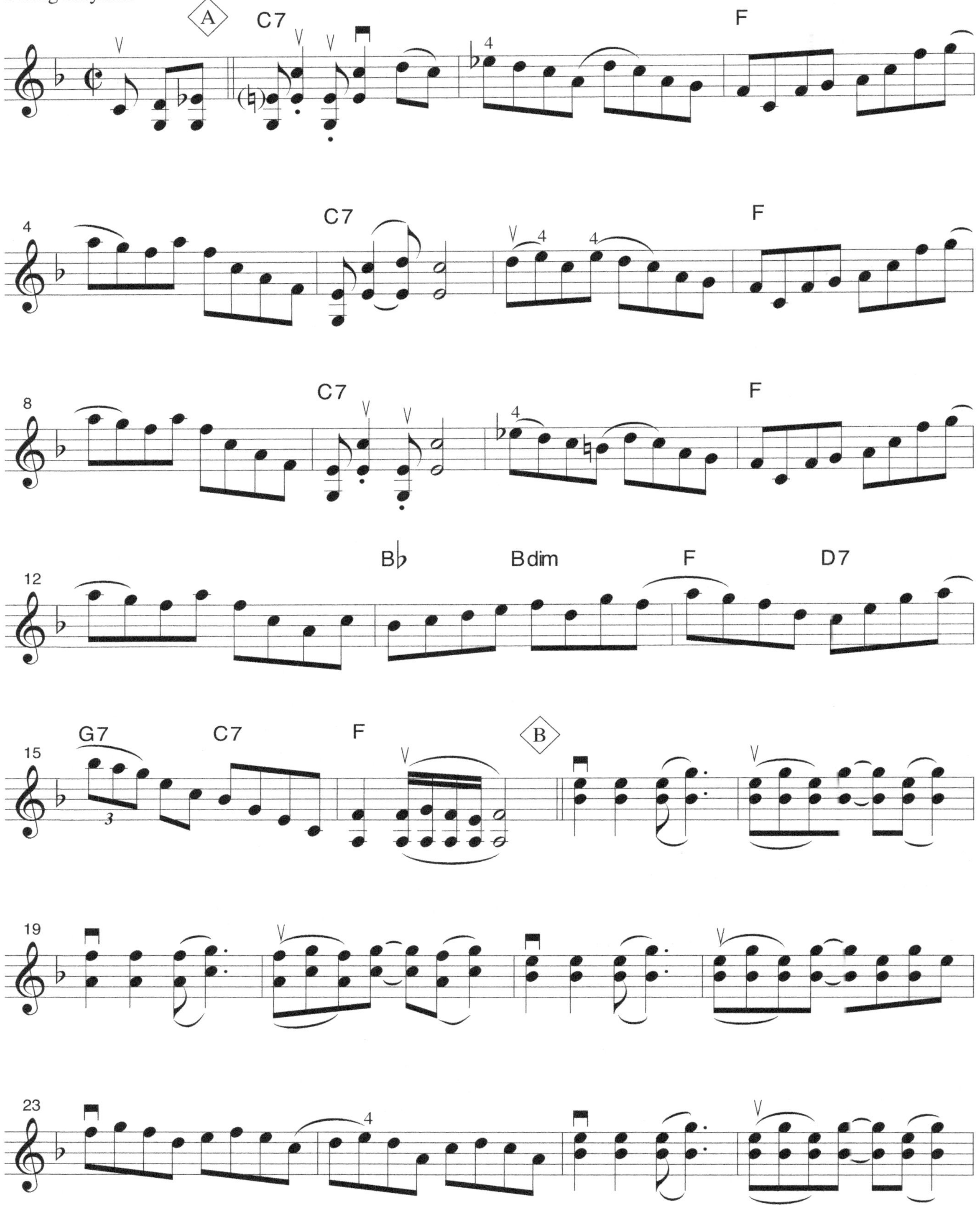

*Slide finger one quarter tone down and back.

In the style of Loretta Brank

# Wild John

This version is based on the playing of Terry Morris.

Traditional

*In the style of Terry Morris*

# Velvet's Waltz

*Velvet's Waltz* is presented in two different versions.
The first is the basic melody and the second is a more advanced
version which is based on the playing of Herman Johnson.

Swing Rhythm

Dale Morris
(Used by Permission)

TRACK 42

# Shuckin' the Bush

This tune may also be known as C*huck in the Bush*. Fiddlers often start with the ⟨E⟩ section before the ⟨A⟩ section.

Traditional

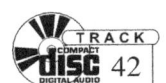

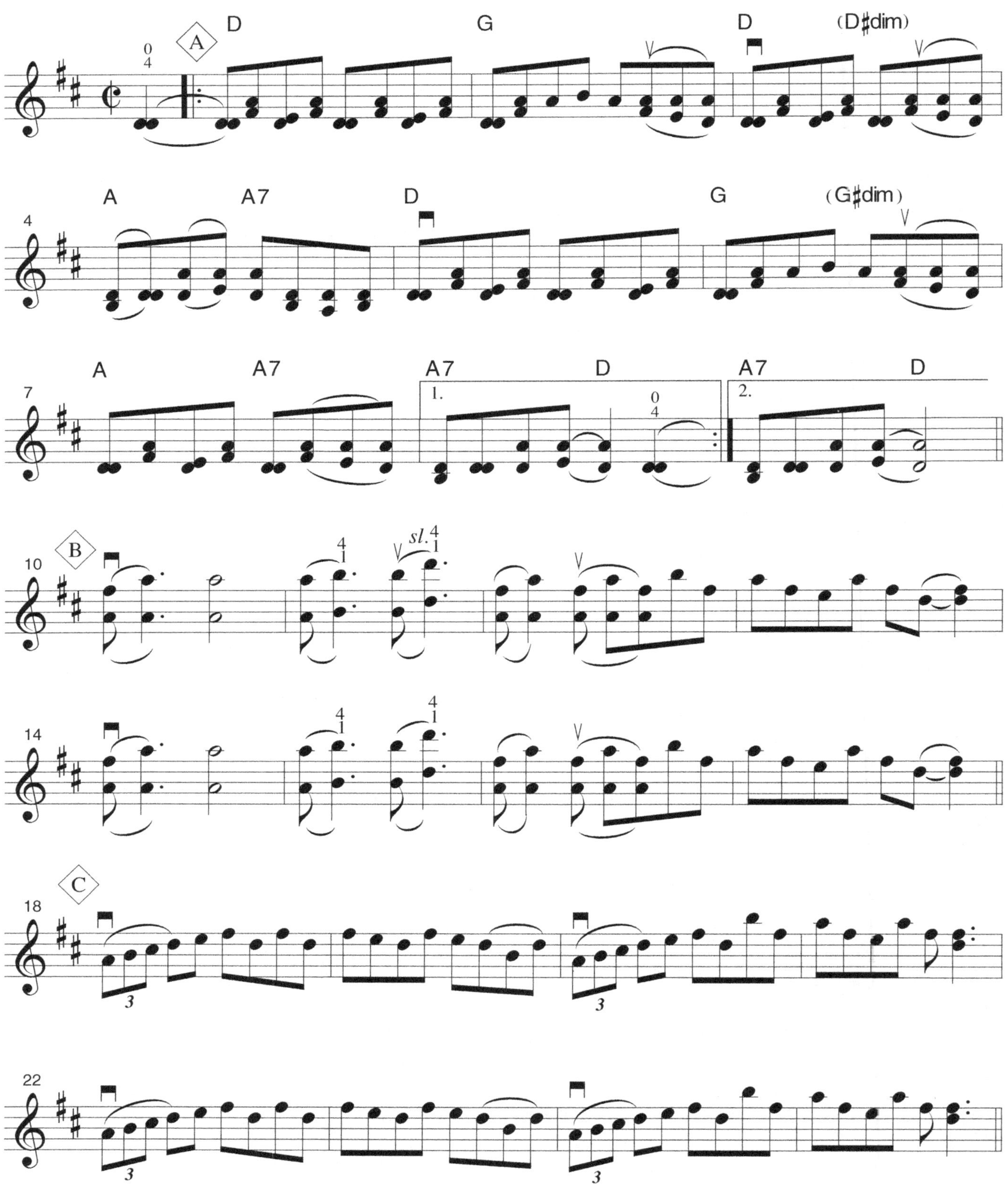

*In the style of Herman Johnson*

TRACK 43

# Cotton Patch Rag

Swing Rhythm

Arthur Smith

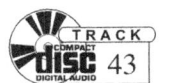

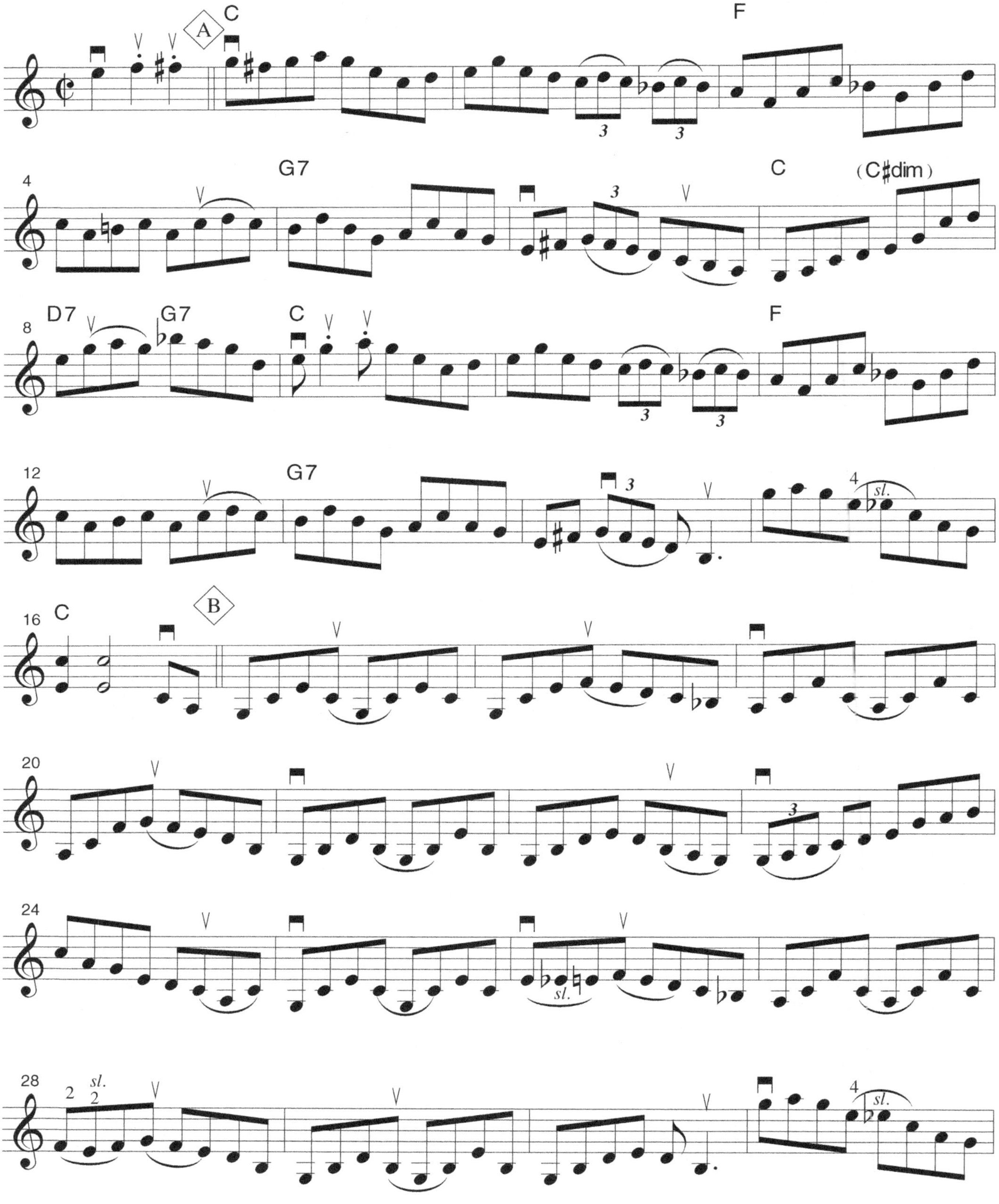

# Crafton's Blues

*In the style of Herman Johnson*

# Durang's Hornpipe

TRACK 45

This tune is a good contest hoedown. The ⟨E⟩ section is not part of the original song, but is a fun variation.

Traditional

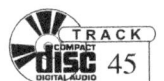

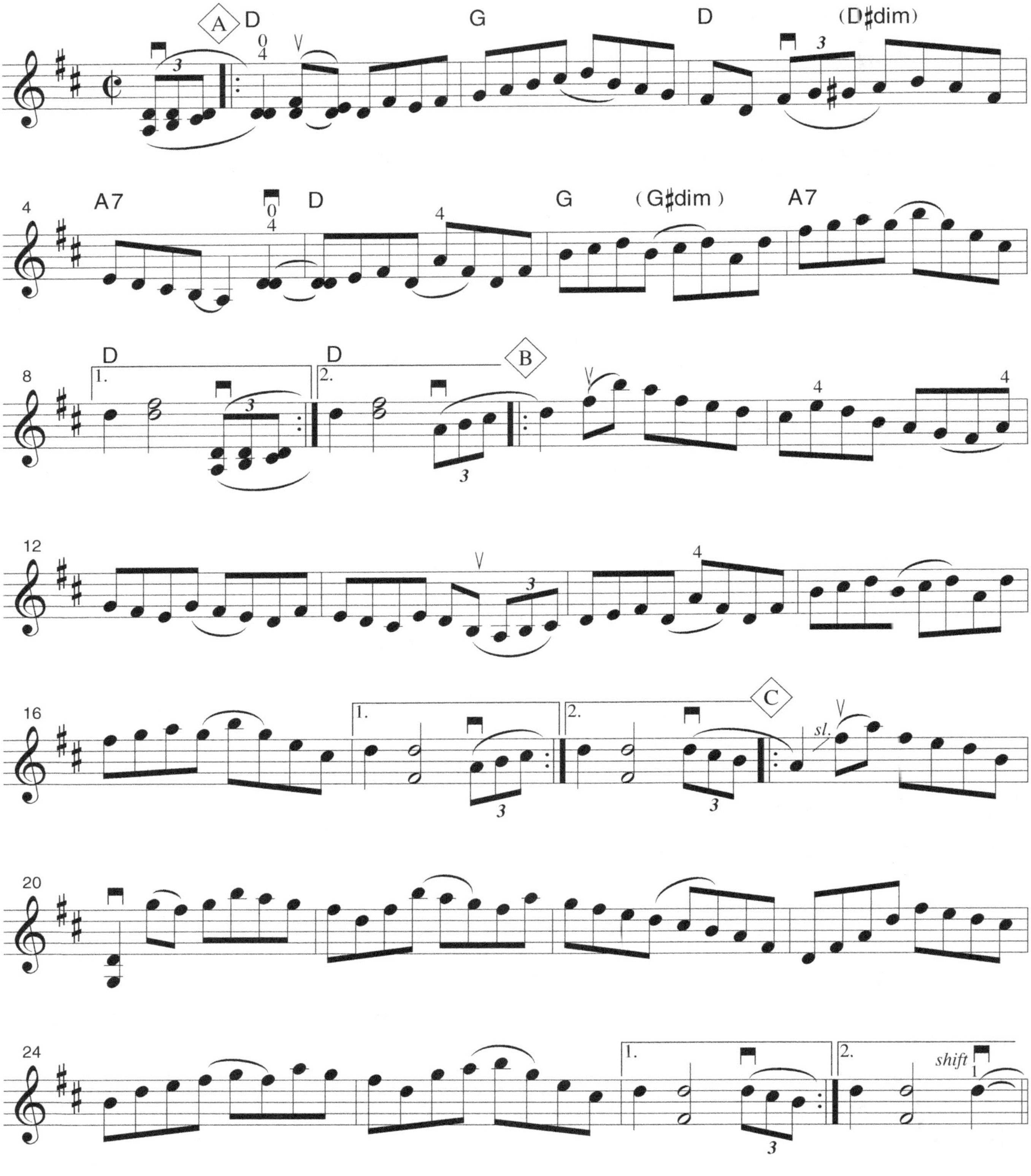

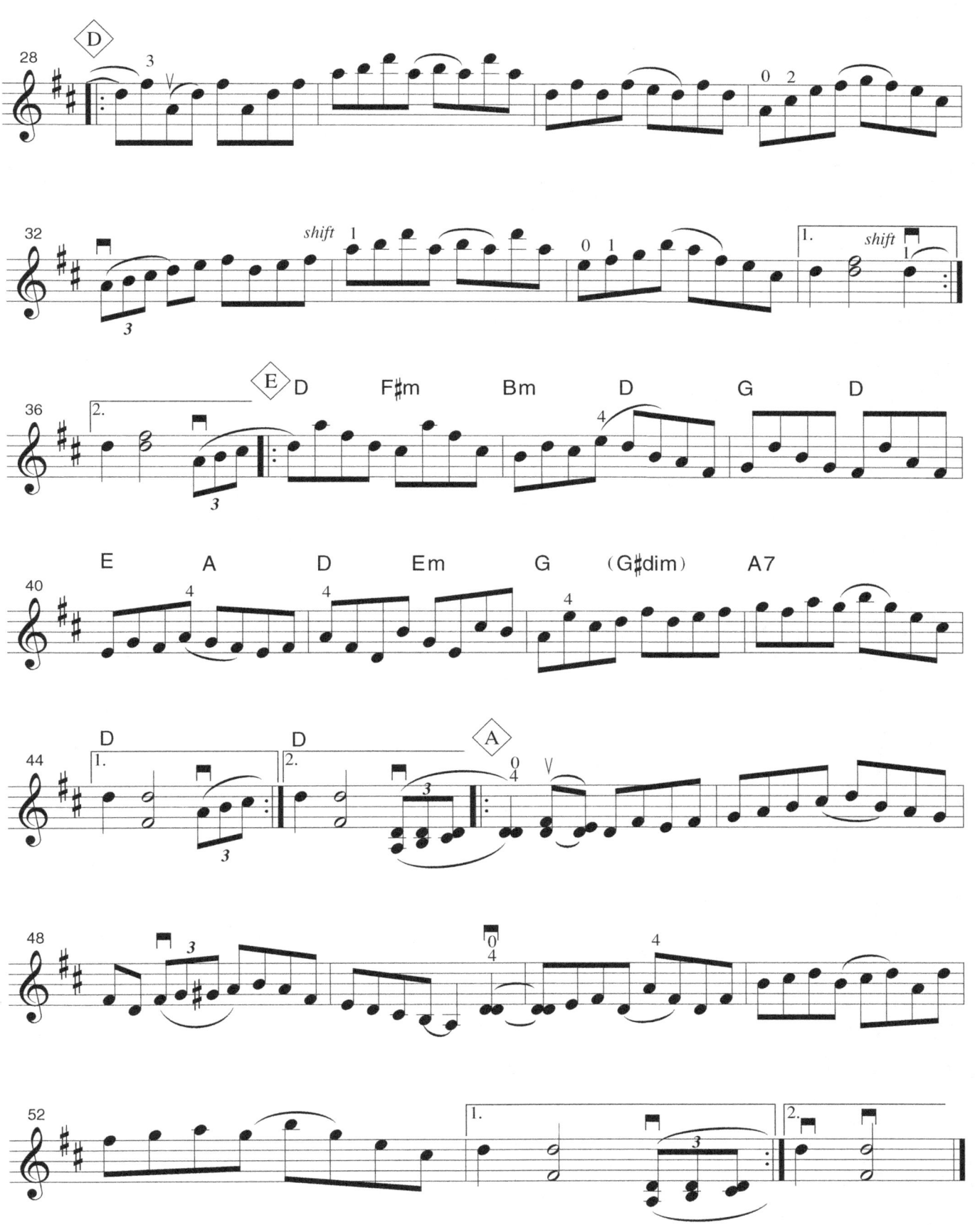

*In the style of Herman Johnson*

# Eva Ann Waltz

Swing Rhythm
(on eighth notes)

This tune uses harmonics (○), which means to shift high and with the 4th finger gently touch the string on the exact place necessary to achieve the stated note with a clear tone.

Frankie Kelly
(Used by Permission)

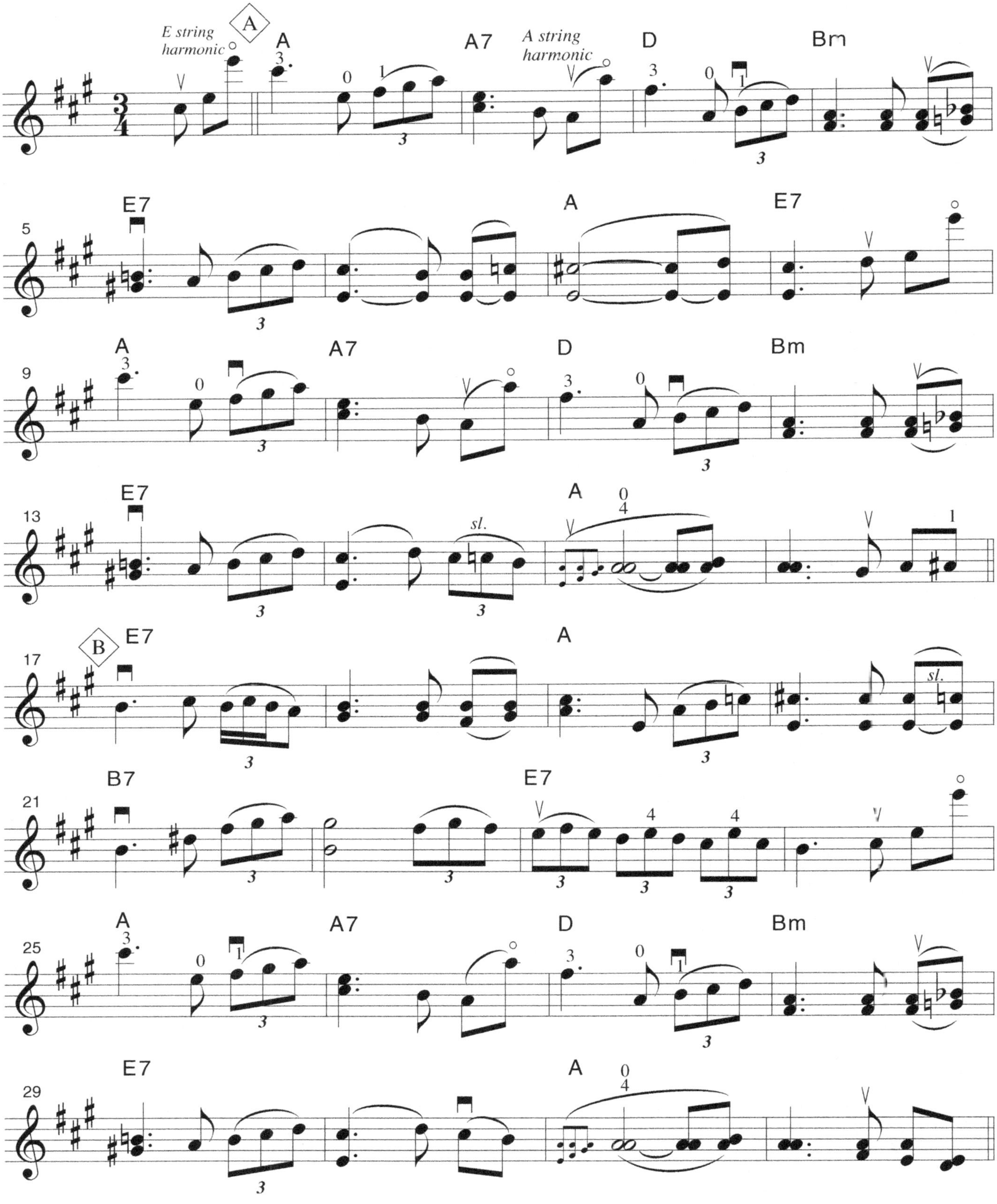

*In the style of Herman Johnson*

# Leather Britches

Traditional

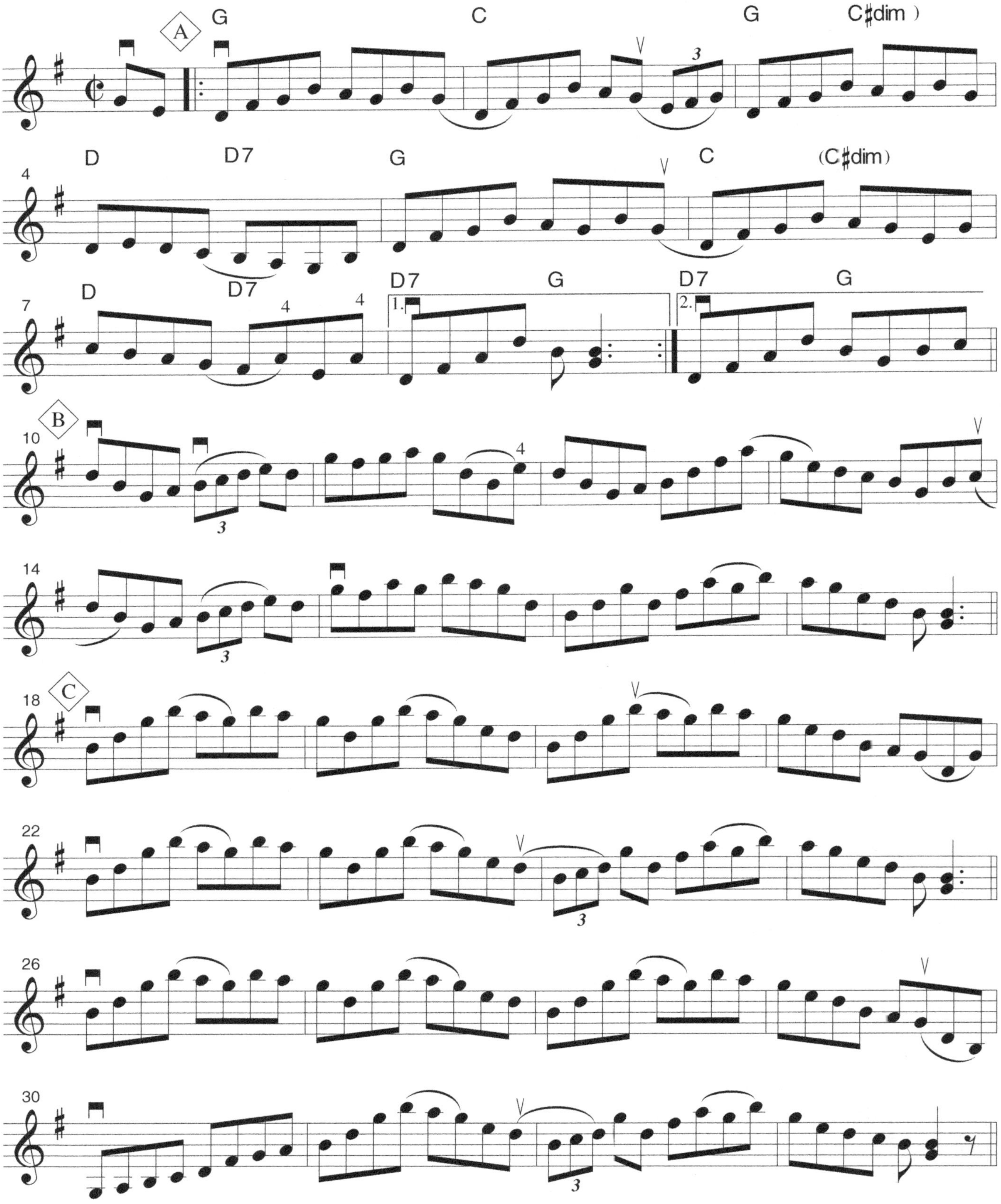

*In the style of Herman Johnson*

# Topeka Polka

Spade Cooley &
Chubby Wise

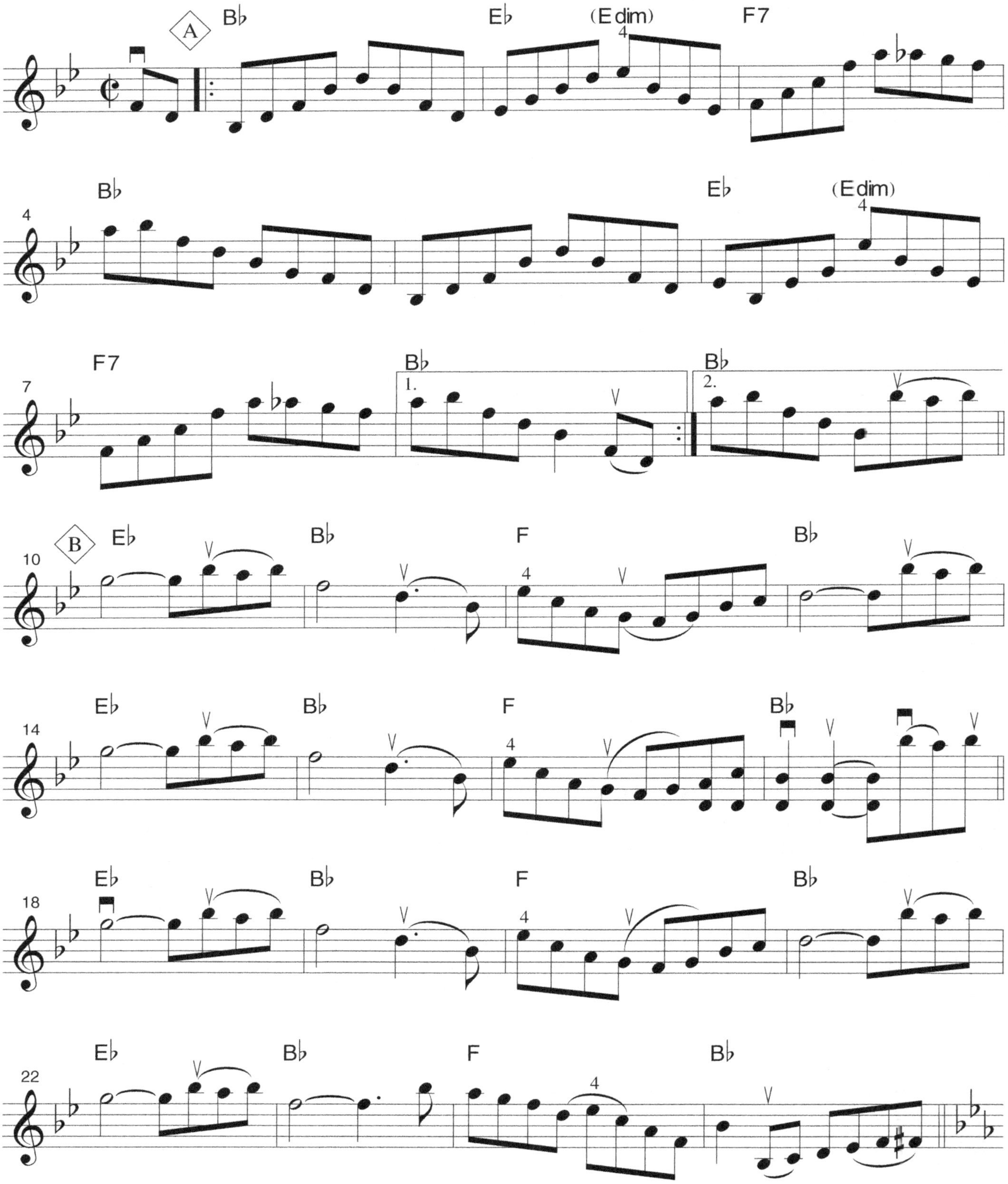

*In the style of Herman Johnson*

# Tom and Jerry

A typical Texas style chord progression is shown.

Traditional

*In the style of Herman Johnson*

# High Level Hornpipe

Traditional (Scottish)

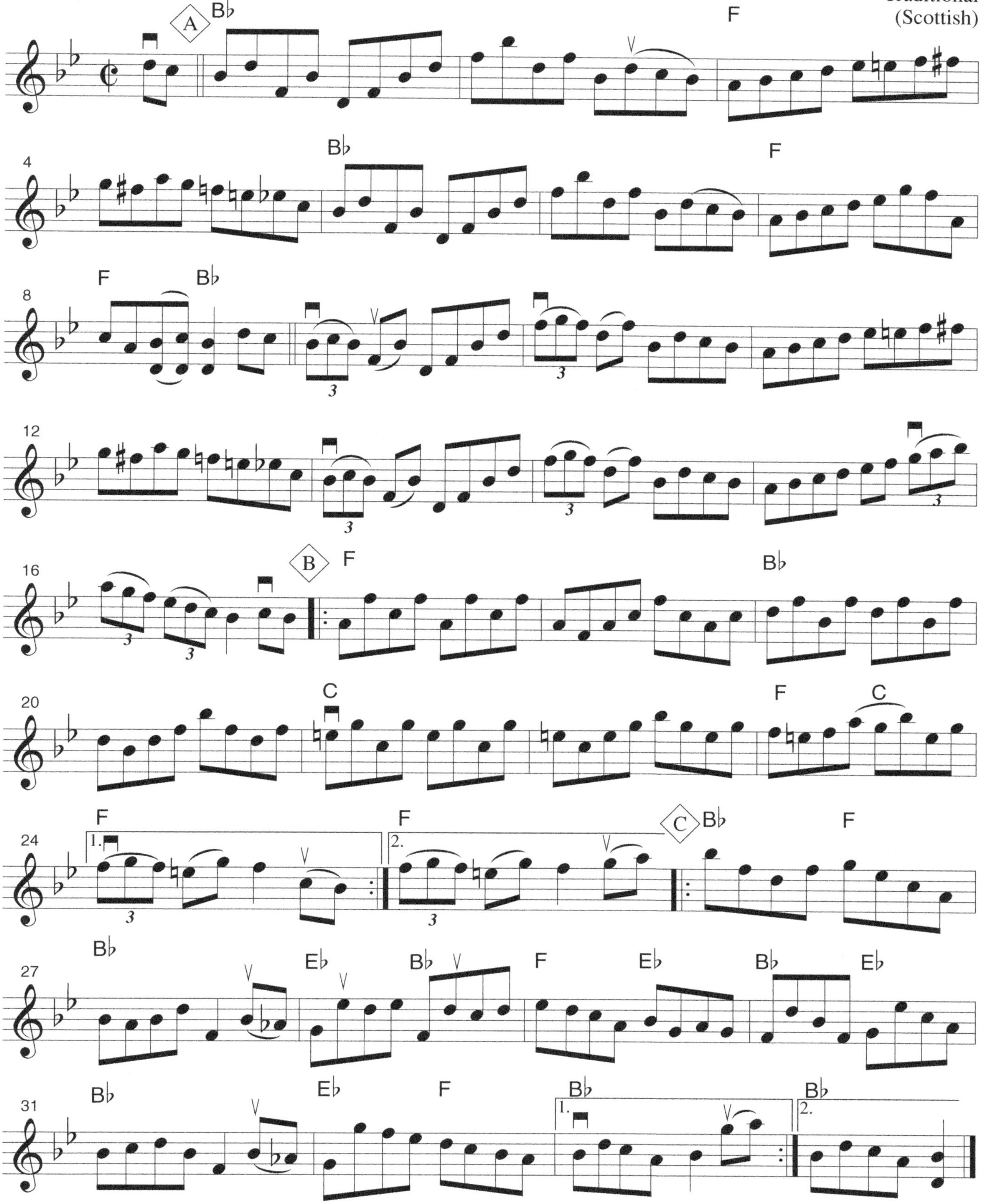

Made in United States
Orlando, FL
12 January 2022

13331882R00046